Presented To:

From:

Date:

# Real
## Messages *from*
# Heaven

*And Other True Stories of Miracles,*
*Divine Intervention, and Supernatural Occurrences*

# Faye Aldridge

DESTINY IMAGE® PUBLISHERS, INC.

P.O. Box 310, Shippensburg, PA 17257-0310

*"Promoting Inspired Lives."*

This book and all other Destiny Image, Revival Press, MercyPlace, Fresh Bread, Destiny Image Fiction, and Treasure House books are available at Christian bookstores and distributors worldwide.

For a U.S. bookstore nearest you, call **1-800-722-6774**.

For more information on foreign distributors, call **717-532-3040**.

Reach us on the Internet: **www.destinyimage.com**.

ISBN 13 TP: 978-0-7684-4047-8

ISBN 13 Ebook: 978-0-7684-8879-1

For Worldwide Distribution, Printed in the U.S.A.

1 2 3 4 5 6 / 14 13 12 11

# Dedication

To my heavenly Father,
My children, Donna and David,
My grandchildren, Jacob, Daniel, and Reese,
and
in loving memory of
Burke Aldridge.

# Acknowledgments

To Dr. Carl Willis and Dr. Arthur Cushman who made me aware of their amazing encounters with my deceased husband, Burke Aldridge; I acknowledge my gratitude. It took courage for each of you to tell me what you saw and heard! Thanks for allowing me to write about your experiences. Our heavenly Father designed your experiences and inspired me to write this book.

To each of the people who allowed me to write about their incredible experiences and encounters, I am grateful for you opening your lives so that others might be encouraged and receive hope by reading about your experiences.

I offer my thanks to long time friends Mildred Barrett and Phyllis Carman for their prayers and encouragement during the writing of this book.

# Contents

*Oh give thanks to the Lord, call upon His name; make known His deeds among the peoples. Sing to Him, sing praises to Him; speak of all His wonders. Glory in His holy name; let the heart of those who seek the Lord be glad. Seek the Lord and His strength; seek His face continually. Remember His wonderful deeds which He has done... For great is the Lord, and greatly to be praised...* (1 Chronicles 16:8-12,25).

# Letter

Over 30 years ago, I heard Elisabeth Kubler-Ross, author of the groundbreaking book, *On Death and Dying,* speak to several hundred people in Louisville, Kentucky, about her studies concerning "near-death experiences" and her then recent studies on "life after death." She described herself as a "pessimistic Protestant" before her studies on death and after-death experiences. She stated that since her research, she had become convinced without a doubt there was definitely life after death. This was a very powerful moment for me personally to hear one who was a psychiatrist by training make such a statement not based on faith, but on scientific research.

I experienced another powerful moment several months ago when Faye Aldridge, a person whom I had never met before, entered my office at the hospital and told me a story about her husband. Two doctors who work at this hospital had seen him after his death. It was an incredible experience for them, for her, and for her family. This experience led her to write a book about her husband's after-death appearance and similar experiences. She feels she received a special blessing from God and so do I. She wants to share this blessing with us.

This book is not research, but it does contain extraordinary stories, which have come from the mouths of those who have experienced these events. I hope this book will be a source of hope and peace as you read these words and reflect on the stories. Life is a mystery, but sometimes the mystery comes to us face to face to reassure us of the unknown. I applaud the work of Faye Aldridge and I hope this book will minister to those who read it.

Lewis M. Lamberth, Jr.

Director of Pastoral Services

Baptist Hospital

Nashville, Tennessee

# Chapter 1

# A Fax From Heaven

"Every once in a while, something happens to you that you just can't explain. You know, when all you can do is take pause or stand still in complete awe...that night between 11:30 and 12:00, as I sat alone on the couch in my family room, something happened. Initially I was frightened and uneasy, only to be overcome, just as suddenly, by a sense of peace and calmness like I have never known before. There was a translucent form there, which I did not recognize. Then I heard a voice, which I had heard before, say, 'I have gone to Heaven to be with God. Don't worry about me, I am OK.' I knew that voice. I didn't need to call the hospital to find out that Mr. Aldridge had gone on to be with God, just as he had said."

The preceding paragraph is an excerpt from a letter written by Dr. Carl Willis, a Nashville oncologist. Dr. Willis was stunned when a deceased patient appeared in his living room and spoke to him. Later, he learned he was not the only physician who experienced an after-death appearance from Burke Aldridge.

My husband, Burke, had been under a physician's care for months; suffering from continuous pain had become a way of life for him, but the source of the pain remained a mystery. On a cold February night in 2005,

I rushed him to the emergency room at Baptist Hospital in Nashville, Tennessee. His pain had reached an unbearable level and was accompanied by acute respiratory distress.

The emergency staff responded at once when they realized the severity of Burke's symptoms. His right lung had collapsed. Within minutes, the nurse started him on oxygen and administered an injection of morphine to lessen the severe chest pain. Burke was admitted to the critical care unit, a unit reserved for only the most life-threatening conditions.

For the next five days, Burke's body was probed, biopsied, scanned, and X-rayed. The pain never decreased and his inability to breathe became nearly unbearable. It was hard to believe this critically ill man had been busy living an active life only days before. Now my strong, 53-year-old husband slipped in and out of consciousness, engaged in a battle for his life.

I did all I could to make him comfortable. He knew how much I loved him, and I assured him that I would remain by his side. I prayed for him, and I read Scripture to him even when he was not conscious. I knew his spirit had to remain strong in order to fight the attack against his body.

On the sixth day, the biopsy results confirmed the worst: Burke had lung cancer, and it had spread to his spine. He was in the fourth and final stage with a life expectancy of only 30 days. Burke calmly listened to the ominous prognosis, then looked at me and said, "Where is the fear? It's strange but there is no fear." I understood and agreed with him because I was also free of fear. We both knew God was with us in the midst of the chaos and we were extremely grateful for His presence.

How do you tell your children you are dying? How do you find the right words?

As a father, Burke was amazing! From day one, he participated in the care of our son and daughter, David and Donna. When they were babies, he rocked them to sleep and fed them as often as I did. When they were young children, he nurtured them and played games with them. Burke always had the unique ability to see life through their eyes, never expecting them to see life through his. As the children grew, they often sang and played guitar with their dad. Our family loved, laughed, and was openly affectionate. We were happy together, and it was too soon to say good-bye.

The evening after we had received the doctor's prognosis, our children arrived at the hospital. I sat nearby and listened as Burke told them the dreadful news. A feeling of helplessness crushed me as I watched them attempt to control their emotions. Tears welled in their eyes and spilled over in silence as they tried to be strong for their dad. We had never experienced that kind of pain before. I could almost hear their hearts break. I felt as if a part of me was dying.

It was Burke's nature to find the good in any situation, a quality that did not fail him even in that terrible moment of realization. Gently, Burke told the children how wonderful it was to love them, to be their dad, and to have shared their life with them. He spoke plainly to them of the importance of faith in our Lord. He reminded them to look past this temporary life toward the approaching life eternal, where the word good-bye does not exist. He expressed his desire that God would use the situation and cause something good to come from his premature death.

It was late when David and Donna went home, and I settled down in a chair, wanting to sleep—to escape reality. Burke's breathing was difficult. He was in excruciating pain and restless in the unfamiliar hospital bed. It was a night filled with bittersweet emotions. We all lived through that day, but I believe it was the most heartrending day we ever endured.

The following days and nights turned into a blur of continuous mental and physical anguish. Family and friends came for brief visits. They came to say good-bye to a very deserving and special person whose life appeared to be drawing to a close. Outside the door, they wept and then dried their eyes before entering the room.

Burke bravely faced his last days, though weary from relentless pain and the ever-present struggle to breathe. He described his intense pain as half-physical and half-heartsick pain. Leaving his loved ones caused him great distress. As others hid their tears, so did I. I hid them well in an attempt to spare him even more pain. He could not bear to think of leaving me alone, so I pretended I was a rock even when I felt like a pebble.

The morning of February 28, day 22 of Burke's final journey, began with a fine, cold rain. Gray clouds hovered over the city. I stood by his bed watching him sleep and listening to each breath. He was heavily sedated. For the moment, I was thankful he was not hurting.

Suddenly, Burke's eyes opened and he smiled a radiant smile! He told me he had been with the Lord! He said the Lord had showed him things of Heaven and spoke to him about them. With great peace, Burke told me, "The Lord said I can come home and He will help me cross over." My husband reminded me that his quality of life had diminished to the point where he was no longer living, merely existing in agony. With no hesitation and an unmistakable anticipation, Burke told me he was ready to go. I could no longer hide my tears, and they fell down my face. He smiled at me and said, "No regrets." My heart was breaking, but I nodded and agreed, "No regrets."

I did not give up at that time, but I did give in. I accepted God's will. I knew Burke was in God's hands, and His will would soon be done. My prayers changed; I no longer prayed for Burke to stay on earth. I promised him I would remain beside him and hold his hand until Jesus took his other hand to lift him up to Heaven. He assured me that he would meet me there when it was my turn to cross over.

In a short time, the Lord allowed me to keep my promise; I held Burke's hand as his life on earth ended later that same day. Death came for him just before midnight. As I held Burke's hand in mine, I became aware of a holy presence. Although it was beyond my physical sight, I knew beyond doubt that an angelic presence saturated the very atmosphere of the room. There was a strong feeling of anticipation in the air as Burke's spirit left his body. If I had reached above my head, I believe I could have touched the angels! In my spirit, I could hear them rejoicing, "Burke's coming home, Burke's coming home!" I found comfort in the knowledge that his life in Heaven was about to begin.

I called our children after Burke died, and they came to say good-bye. We left the hospital just before three o'clock in the morning as giant, unpredicted snowflakes blanketed the streets. Snow was not in the forecast; however, Burke had repeatedly mentioned seeing snow the day before. Against the wishes of the children, I drove home alone. I had to reconcile within my heart the reality of my situation.

My strength was gone. Exhaustion and loneliness overwhelmed me. I could barely see the road because the snowfall was so heavy. It took me almost an hour to get to our home in the country. Darkness accentuated the lonely music made by wind chimes swaying in the cold, winter wind.

I drove into the garage and pressed the remote, closing the garage door. It closed partially then raised right back up. It closed successfully on the second try. I did not think it was significant until the same thing happened the next two nights when I entered the garage. Each time, it was as if someone walked into the garage behind me, triggering the safety device. I saw no one.

I slept about three hours before David came over at 8 A.M. As soon as he arrived, the phones began to ring. David answered but heard only a dial tone. The ringing continued as he moved from phone to phone all through the house. The answering machine was set to answer after four rings; however, the answering machine did not respond, though it was in perfect working condition. All the phones in the house were ringing! The ringing stopping after a dozen rings. Suddenly, I remembered—Burke said he was going to try to send me a fax when he got to Heaven letting me know he was all right. I said as much to David. He bounded up the stairs to my office and discovered the fax machine was unplugged! We shook our heads in disbelief, uncertain of what just happened.

Two days later, Dr. Arthur Cushman, a neurosurgeon, and his wife, Carolyn, visited our family at the funeral home. Dr. Cushman called me aside and told me a miraculous, unusual report—Burke had appeared in his home the night before, nearly 24 hours after his death! He said Burke appeared to him in the center of a white light. He described what he saw: *"Burke's body was surrounded by a white light like a white halo. He looked very healthy and happy and appeared to be younger than at the time of his death."*

Burke spoke to him saying, *"Don't worry, Slim, I'm all right."* (Slim was a nickname Burke had called him for many years.) Dr. Cushman continued, *"He then gradually faded out of sight. There was no one else with him, but I could tell he was in a beautiful land filled with flowers; I could see the flowers behind him. This is the only time I have ever had an experience like that. I sure am glad that Burke came to tell me good-bye!"*

My family and I welcomed this news as a rare gift from God. We knew Burke was a Christian and we believed he was in Heaven. The news of Burke's after-death appearance to Dr. Cushman was a welcome source of encouragement. My family and I gained strength when we learned of the encounter. Amazement and appreciation filled me in response to the Lord's generous gift. I sensed that God was reminding me, "I am with you; you are never alone."

Less than two weeks later, I had a conversation with Dr. Willis, Burke's oncologist. He, too, had a story to tell. He told me Burke visited him in his home on the very night he died! Dr. Willis reported he was in his family room reading a book that night. He saw something unusual in his peripheral vision—a shimmering white light. As he refocused his eyes, the light began to manifest into the shape of a man's body. Dr. Willis could not clearly see the man's face because the man was translucent. Dr. Willis was astounded when he heard Burke's voice say, *"I have gone to Heaven to be with God. Don't worry about me. I am OK."*

Dr. Willis said in a letter to me, *"I knew that voice. I didn't need to call the hospital to find out that Mr. Aldridge had gone on to be with God, just as he had said. He was ready for the Lord, and the Lord was ready for him, despite my intentions. I think he must have known how much I wanted to help him, and he stopped by just to let me know he was feeling a whole lot better. He was breathing a lot better and he had no more pain. He had met a better Doctor who had given him rest and comfort and had granted him everlasting life. I hope this recap of my encounter brings comfort to you."*

I asked Dr. Willis and Dr. Cushman for written documentation of the encounters. Both physicians were kind enough to comply with my request. Dr. Cushman faxed a letter to me on March 29, 2005, and Dr. Willis faxed his letter to me on March 31, 2005. I was sitting at my desk reading both letters and contemplating the significance of the content when I realized the true meaning of the letters. I really did get a fax from Heaven! The message that I received from Burke by way of two physicians was, *"I've gone to Heaven to be with God. Don't worry. I am OK!"* Two witnesses confirmed the message!

> *And we know that in all things God works for the good of those who love Him, who have been called according to His purpose* (Romans 8:28 NIV).

# Chapter 2

# A Yellow Rose

I carried two heavy bags of groceries from the garage into the kitchen. The house was quiet. A miniature pink rose had been placed on the counter of the island in the center of our kitchen. A small square of folded white paper rested behind the beautiful rose. I picked up the note and smiled as I read: "To say I love you would be enough, I know; but I'd rather say 'I love you' with a rose." The note was signed, "Love, Burke."

I placed the rose in a small vase of water, tucked the little note in my wallet between my library and voter registration cards, and then promptly forgot about the heartwarming little gift.

I absolutely love flowers and they were a recurring theme in our marriage; beginning with the beautiful gardenias that filled the church on the day of our wedding. The fragrance of the gardenia is sweet, aromatic, and unmistakable. Many times, I have placed a gardenia blossom or a rose bud on my pillow just so I could enjoy the wonderful fragrance as I drifted off to sleep.

Burke had given me flowers on many occasions during our marriage—sometimes roses, sometimes Stargazer lilies; however, he knew yellow roses were my favorite. I always thanked my husband and carried on over his lovely flower gifts. In hindsight, I never appreciated them enough.

My husband died about six months after he gave me the sweet little miniature rose.

In the days that followed Burke's death, flowers came pouring into the funeral home and the church; some were even delivered to our home. Words could never express the depths of my gratitude; each flower meant someone was remembering Burke and that fact deeply touched my heart. Three precious words echoed in my mind each time a floral arrangement was delivered; I suppose as long as I live, flowers will always mean "I love you" to me.

After Burke's funeral, I took many of the beautiful, fresh flowers to my now lonely home. All too soon, the colorful flowers withered and died. When there were no more fresh flowers in the house, I missed them a great deal.

Three weeks after I buried my husband, the florist delivered a unique arrangement to my home. There were so many fresh flowers! The arrangement was nearly three feet high! I have never seen such a glorious, gorgeous array! The large, square, ivory-colored metal container held a fabulous assortment of all kinds of flowers. Purple iris and yellow roses were predominant; they stood out strikingly above all the rest. I opened the envelope that accompanied the flowers to find my friend, Charline Wilhite, had sent them. She purposefully waited to send her gift in memory of Burke, knowing that it would be even more special after all the others had faded and died. I positioned the arrangement in a place of honor—in the center of my long dining table, in front of the kitchen fireplace.

Each morning I sat alone, sipping my coffee next to an empty chair and trying to adapt to my new way of life. I only needed to look up and Charline's flowers gave me a bit of comfort. They spoke those same three words to my broken heart: "I love you." I am quite certain Charline never realized how much her gift meant to me during those early days of brokenness. I tried to express my gratitude, but my words were never quite adequate.

As the days passed, one by one, the flowers drooped and died. Each day, I removed the dead ones, leaving the live ones in ample water. Finally, the day came when all the flowers were gone. Only the greenery remained alive, except for one yellow rose. I stopped adding water to the container, but, surprisingly, the gorgeous, perfectly formed little rose did not droop and it did not fade. After a month, I removed the rose from the greenery and laid it on the mantle.

Though the rose remained on the mantle for many weeks and became dry to the touch, the color remained vibrant, its head never drooped, and the petals never withered! Thinking the little yellow rose must have been treated with a preservative, I carried it with me and visited the florist to find what they had done to make it stay so perfect. Each employee looked at it and admired the rose, but no one had an explanation. One man, presumably the owner, said he had never seen a rose remain so perfectly preserved. He told me only God could do such a thing! He suggested I store it in a sealed glass container in order to keep it safe.

One day, I was sorting out the cards in my wallet and a folded, square piece of white paper fell out. I picked it up and unfolded it. Once again I read, "To say I love you would be enough, I know; but I'd rather say 'I love you' with a rose. Love, Burke." Could it be? He had been in Heaven for months! Was the strange little rose his way of saying, "I love you"?

Many years have passed and the little rose remains the same—its vibrant, yellow petals are  fully opened and the stem is still green.

Since Burke died, I have learned to accept the gifts and not question the Giver. I hear Him say, "I love you" each time I look at the extraordinary yellow rose that never died.

# Chapter 3

# Slow Motion

When I was a little girl growing up in rural Mississippi, I was involved in a very serious car accident. At the age of 10, I was assigned the chore of grocery shopping one Saturday morning. At that early age, I knew what to buy and what not to buy, and I made no exceptions! We had very little money. My father died at the age of 25 leaving three children under the age of five to be cared for by my mother. We did not own a car and town was two miles away. Mama seized the opportunity when the landowner where we lived and worked offered me a ride that morning.

I rode in the back seat of Mr. Landrum's new Plymouth, and I don't remember saying a word on the trip to town. My list was short and simple; I completed the shopping and placed the groceries in the trunk of the car for the ride home. My grandmother who lived near us rode in the back seat with me, and a cousin rode on the front seat with Mr. Landrum.

Central Mississippi is mostly flat land; however, there was a hill on the outskirts of town to the north. We began our descent down that hill, and something frightening happened. The car swerved from one side of the road to the other! I recall Mr. Landrum shouting, "I can't steer it! It won't stop!" The car careened from one shoulder of the road to the other as the car picked up speed going down the hill approaching the bridge that spanned Box's Creek. Strangely and fortunately, there were no other cars in sight at the moment.

There were no seat belts to restrain us, so we tossed from side to side as the car closed the distance between us and the bridge abutments of Box's Creek Bridge. The road was built up high to protect it from the creek overflow during heavy rains and that elevation created an element of danger.

Just before we reached the bridge abutment, Mr. Landrum overcompensated and jerked the steering wheel hard to the left! We missed the bridge abutment and made a complete U-turn, which led us to the edge of the road where we began our descent. The car tumbled over and over and over until it came to rest against a row of trees and a barbed wire fence adjacent to a cotton field.

Divine intervention surely saved us! First, there were no cars in sight. Second, we did not hit the solid concrete bridge abutment. Third, we were not injured in the wreck. God's merciful power and angels filled that car, as real as the air we breathed! God left proof of His presence in the mind of a child. I remember how the car made a complete revolution several times, yet we did not crash against the glass or metal, as we logically should have. Somehow, God enclosed us in a safe place within the car, surrounded by more angels than I could count, in the form of sparkling particles of light!

From the moment we left the road, life changed! *We were in slow motion!* Inside the car on that particular day, we appeared to be weightless and *the laws of gravity no longer seemed to apply*. I felt no distress as my body tumbled in unison with the tumbling automobile! I was not injured when my head slowly impacted the ceiling of the car as it rolled over and over.

I distinctly remember seeing small sparkling particles of light floating before my curious eyes. They were everywhere, all around us! My mind focused on the tiny light particles. I saw each one separately as one sees snowflakes drifting separately on a snowy winter day. Each tiny particle of light appeared to be unique and different. I was not fearful for my life. I was calm, and my thoughts were simply *wow, wow,* and *wow!*

When the car landed upright, we managed to crawl out of it even though the top was crushed. We walked away unharmed!

In recent days, I have heard others tell about seeing the same sparkling particles of light in times of crisis. It seems the light particles have the ability to separate into tiny sparkling particles or cluster together, forming an obvious halo or one solid mass of light. I have come to understand that the light particles must be God's angels! Apparently, they come in all shapes and sizes! That is the only explanation I have for what I saw and experienced during the accident! The angels surrounded us that day, as plentiful as feathers in a pillow. They protected us from a wreck that logically should have killed everyone inside the car.

> *The angel of the Lord encamps around those who fear Him, and rescues them* (Psalm 34:7).

# Chapter 4

# Go Back

Barbara and Jerry Brantley were happily married. They lived in Grand Bay, Alabama, with their five-year-old son. As a child growing up in rural Mississippi, my sister Barbara dreamed of living near the ocean. Her home so close to the Gulf of Mexico was a dream come true. Barbara enjoyed every minute of her life and had no inclination to be anywhere else.

It was the summer of 1977. Jerry and Barbara often played golf together on the weekends at a country club not far from their home. One beautiful, weekend day, the couple looked forward to a relaxing afternoon on the links. Jerry left first in his own car, with Andy, their son, in the back seat. Barbara had plans for later that day, so she followed closely in her own vehicle.

As the little caravan rounded a curve on the winding road, an oncoming car crossed into Barbara's lane. (The driver later claimed she veered into oncoming traffic because the sun obscured her view.) The large Pontiac Bonneville hit Barbara's compact VW Rabbit head-on. Having neglected to wear a seatbelt, Barbara was unrestrained; the impact threw her body across the car. With great force, her head, neck, and back struck the metal strip between the front and rear passenger-side windows.

Five-year-old Andy witnessed the crash from the rear window of his dad's car. Jerry brought his car to a screeching halt and was at the scene of the accident within minutes. It was obvious Barbara had sustained major injuries; the back of her head was laid open from top to bottom. Jerry suspected her neck was broken and tried to stabilize her until an ambulance arrived. Little Andy was traumatized.

Singing River Hospital in Pascagoula provided emergency care. In addition to the massive head trauma, Barbara had sustained a broken collarbone and, as Jerry feared, a fractured cervical spine at two levels— her neck was broken in two places!

In order to stabilize Barbara's neck and, hopefully, prevent paralysis, doctors attached her head to a traction device designed to hold her firmly in a stable position. The procedure required to attach the device was frightening. A nurse shaved Barbara's head and an orthopedic surgeon drilled a hole in her skull above each ear. Metal tongs were attached directly into her skull with a weighted cable attached. The contraption created a pulley device that held Barbara's head like a vise.

Barbara was in excruciating pain as her condition deteriorated. Her vital signs became unstable until, finally, Barbara stopped breathing. For a brief time, Barbara's injuries seemed to have taken her life.

Barbara will never forget the things she saw during her short interval of death. She remembers she entered a distinctly round tunnel through which she traveled at jet-speed. The tunnel was a beam of light and she became part of the radiant stream. Her body was weightless and totally pain-free. Though she saw no one in the tunnel, she was aware of a presence traveling with her. When she reached the tunnel's end, she exited and saw her husband's deceased grandparents sitting in rocking chairs on a long porch. They were smiling at her. However, they had their hands extended, palms out and up, indicating she was to, "Stop, and go back. Go back!"

Suddenly, and with an agonizing jolt, Barbara returned to her body, experiencing the excruciating pain from which she had escaped while in the beam of light.

Barbara endured the interminably long recovery process bravely, refusing to give up. She could not imagine leaving her young son without a mother, so she fought hard to live. A permanent halo replaced the cranial tongs. The halo was mounted onto her skull then connected to a body cast, enclosing her body from the top of her shoulders to her hips. She wore the cast and halo for the next four months while her fractured cervical spine healed. Barbara's recovery was slow and required much patience and determination. But recover she did. More than 30 years later, Barbara still enjoys life with minimal deficits, considering the nature of the injuries she endured. She still clearly recalls her journey through the beaming stream of light. Barbara no longer fears death; she had a brief preview of what waits on the other side!

Chapter 5

# More Than a Dream

Autumn finally arrived. My husband, Burke, and I busied ourselves making plans to go out of state for a weeklong business convention. Our two children, Donna and David, were in elementary school, but we arranged for them to leave school for one week. We planned to drive them to the home of Burke's parents in central Mississippi. The kids would stay there while we flew from Jackson, Mississippi, to the West Coast.

Two weeks before our departure date, I had a disturbing dream. The details of the dream remained vivid in my mind. In the dream, I was a spectator. I usually dreamed in color; however, that time was in black and white. I stood away from the scene watching the circumstances unfold, as one would watch a ball game from the bleachers. I was not capable of entering the scene by speaking or walking into it; I could only stand by and watch.

The first thing I saw was a woman standing with her back toward me. She appeared to be me. She looked upward at a small box. The box appeared to hang as if suspended in the air by an invisible hand!

I watched as the woman wept; she dropped to her knees and fell forward to where her face was against the ground. In anger she struck the ground with her hands and she cried as if her heart would break.

I felt her pain! Her cries became my cries, and her grief became my grief. I ached and knew we were experiencing the same emotions. I looked intently at the suspended box. I shuddered when I realized it was not just a box; it was a tiny casket! I knew the woman's child was in that casket. I was overwhelmed with emotion when I thought I was watching myself out there. Somehow, I experienced grief, brokenness, and a sense of helplessness. I had never experienced anything like that in my entire life.

The dream faded from sight, and I awoke literally shivering. I quietly made my way down the hall to David and Donna's bedrooms. I gently touched their cheeks and kissed them as they slept. I thanked God they were safe in their beds. I went back and forth from room to room. I did not want to let them out of my sight.

I assumed I had a nightmare. I told my husband about the dream the next day, and explained I felt like I had received some kind of warning to safeguard the kids even more than we usually did. Somehow, I knew it was more than a dream. I believed the dream was symbolic of what was to come in the days ahead.

Two weeks passed, and we were indecisive about canceling the trip. The children were healthy, happy, and looking forward to the mini-vacation with their grandparents. The plane tickets were in hand. I told myself I was silly to let a dream affect me that way! We decided to go ahead with our plans.

On Sunday night, we arrived at our destination and checked into our hotel. I could not shake the feelings of impending danger. We made it through Monday and my apprehension grew worse. A gentle pressure invaded my thinking, and the pressure did not let up. My husband shared my apprehension by that time, and he insisted that we should cancel the week and fly to Mississippi the next day, and we did!

We arrived at the home of my in-laws the next evening, and we gathered our children in our arms. On Wednesday, we drove home to

Tennessee. Thursday morning, our schedules returned to normal. I was at work when I received a phone call from my sister in Mobile. I answered my extension, and I heard Barbara call my name. The dream vividly replayed in my mind as I heard her say the words, "Ashley is dead." Once again, I saw that tiny box clearly and dreadfully. The same pain I felt two weeks before in the dream besieged me as I listened to the agony in my sister's voice. She told me their 13-month-old daughter just drowned in Marie's backyard pool.

While Barbara worked, her best friend Marie cared for Ashley. Ashley began walking when she was nine months old. She was a beautiful baby with golden curls, sparkling blue eyes, and a constant smile! On the day of the accident, Marie thought her son was with Ashley and her son thought his mom was with Ashley. That precious baby girl slipped out of their sight and made her way straight to the pool. She loved to be near the water. When they realized she was missing, it was too late.

We drove to Mobile that same day to be with my sister, her husband, and their young son. I ached inside for the loss of that little angel! When we arrived, I did all I could, but I could do nothing that really made a difference. Ashley's toys, clothes, and photographs were evidence throughout the house that she once lived there. My beautiful little niece was gone. The absence of her sweet baby talk left her loved ones speechless and heartbroken! She was laid to rest in a casket like the one in the dream.

Later, I tried to mentally process the dream. The woman in the dream looked like me; so does my sister. Why did I not think of that? Why did I not call my sister and warn her to take extra precautions with Ashley? Perhaps she would have demanded that Marie fix the gate to the pool instead of just asking her to fix the gate that day. I did not know about the broken gate, but my sister did. If only I had shared the dream! I believed the woman in the dream was me. I never imagined the woman in the dream was my sister.

At that time in my life, I knew *about* God; however, I did not *know* God. There is a huge difference! I did not have a personal relationship with Jesus Christ. I knew about Heaven and hell, but I did not fully comprehend either. I had accepted Jesus as my Savior as a child, but I lived separated from God. I did not honor Him in my life. Even though I prayed during those times, I did not know the meaning of faith, so praying was awkward and empty. I lived my life outside of God's will, so I received little comfort when I prayed. Those days were difficult to say the least.

As a Christian today, I realize Jesus or His angel lifted that precious, innocent baby girl from the pool that day and carried her straight to Heaven. I cannot change circumstances, but I wish I could. What I can do now, is acknowledge messages and warnings from God when they come. They come in the form of dreams, visions, and spiritual prompting. I believe they come by way of the Holy Spirit. They are real godly gifts sent for a reason—and should not be ignored.

The Bible speaks of prophetic dreams and visions as real communication from God. Dreams are as significant today as they were in biblical days. I will never again ignore a dream. I will not try to diminish the significance of a message from the Lord. I will seek His face and His help when I do not understand what He is saying to me. I will trust Him to lead me one step at a time until the answer comes.

> *Then they said to him, "We have had a dream and there is no one to interpret it." Then Joseph said to them, "Do not interpretations belong to God?..."* (Genesis 40:8)

Chapter 6

# The Spirit of Comfort

Dawn Elizabeth Ellison and Chad Allen were married on May 23, 1998, at First United Methodist Church in Lexington, Mississippi.

Before the wedding, Dawn presented her mom with a letter. A portion of it read, "The most important day in my life! Finally, I am going to be someone's wife! My mother, my friend...always there to protect me with your unselfish air. You are truly my angel on earth. Thank you for giving me life. I love you more than you could ever know. Thank you, Mommy!"

Dawn's wedding day was perfect and the heartwarming ceremony was special in every way. The attractive couple fairly beamed their joy. Dawn looked radiant—a vision in glowing white! She wore a long veil and a simple-but-elegant floor-length gown. To complete her lovely attire, she wore a brand-new pair of high-top, navy Converse All-stars! Conventional, Dawn was not!

Dawn was born as the "bonus child" of John and Bonnie Ellison. Dawn's siblings, Gaye, Mike, and Glenda, ages 9 to 15, adored her at first sight and carried her everywhere with them. Dawn thrived with all the attention and loved her brother and sisters dearly. She enjoyed a happy and contented childhood as she grew up in her loving, Christian home.

Dawn was a lovely girl with blond hair and sparkling, brown eyes. Always small for her age, Dawn grew to be a strong, feisty tomboy who wanted things her own way. She was active in sports; she played hard and always played to win. Losing was failure, and failure was not a concept Dawn would ever entertain!

Dawn grew into a talented athlete—first in softball; then in high school, she became a powerful, three-point shooter for her basketball team. In her senior year, Dawn's basketball team won a spot in the finals for the first time in the school's history. When the buzzer sounded on the final quarter of the last game, Dawn sat on the gym floor and cried. It was the end of a treasured chapter in her life.

Truth, honesty, and integrity shaped Dawn's character. She truly cared about others and love was simply her way of life. All through high school, Dawn and Chad, her future husband, worked at a farm supply store. The two of them were invaluable employees, and together they almost ran the store. Dawn graduated from high school with honors then graduated from Holmes Community College with a 4.0 average for which she received a Massey Scholarship. The scholarship covered the entire cost of the rest of her education. When she accepted the scholarship, she signed an agreement promising to give 10 percent of her earnings to help others. The agreement was binding for life!

Dawn consistently and quietly helped others whenever she could, never seeking to receive anything in return.

When Dawn was in college, she developed an eating disorder. She was 5 foot 4 inches and weighed only 100 pounds. She chose to seek the help of a Christian counselor. Dawn began to realize her life was out of control. She made the decision to ask Jesus into her heart as her Lord and Savior. Dawn believed this decision was the best she ever made!

May 1998 was a life-changing month for Dawn—she received her doctorate in pharmacy and married her high school sweetheart. Her new husband, Chad Allen, was in the process of finishing his degree at Mississippi State University, and Dawn accepted a position as a pharmacist in

Mobile, Alabama. The newlyweds planned to see each other on weekends until Chad was free to move to Mobile.

On November 20, 1998, Dawn got up and went to the gym, came home, showered, and left for work. When she failed to show up at the pharmacy, the manager became concerned. Dawn's car was soon discovered just outside the pharmacy doors with the driver's door ajar.

Bonnie and John, Dawn's parents, came home for lunch that day to discover a phone message from Dawn's apartment manager. Their hearts sank as they heard their daughter was missing. The Ellisons contacted Chad and the three of them packed and headed for Mobile.

It was a quiet trip. There was pain in the silence; sadness in the unspoken words. Each one of them knew something painful was just ahead; a pain so dreadful none of them could bear to talk or even think about it.

Dawn's mother, Bonnie, recalls, "We were just south of Hattiesburg, traveling on Highway 98, halfway between Hattiesburg and Mobile, when I experienced something that was unexplainable. This extraordinary feeling descended on me! I felt light, happy, lifted up, and so loved. I experienced God giving me a great big hug. I felt like I had swallowed sunshine! I did not understand what just happened to me; neither could I understand the knowledge that came on the heels of that experience. I knew in my heart that Dawn was dead."

At the same time, a verse from the Bible, Romans 8:26, echoed in Bonnie's mind: *"The Spirit also helps our weakness; for we do not know how to pray as we should, but the Spirit Himself intercedes for us with groanings too deep for words."* Bonnie did not immediately tell John, her husband, what she experienced. When she told him later, John surprised her by admitting he had experienced similar feelings at the same time and the same location! John told her Dawn had actually spoken to him, saying, "Daddy, don't worry about me, I am with Pappy." (Pappy, John's deceased father, had died in 1993.)

Bonnie knew God was preparing her for what was to come. She felt numb and paralyzed emotionally, no longer able to think or pray. The situation was so gut-wrenching her brain nearly shut down. She remembers worrying that Dawn might be cold without her coat in the chilly, November air.

The Ellisons and Chad arrived in Mobile and launched a major search for Dawn. The apartment manager arranged for Dawn's photo to be aired on the ten o'clock news with a request for information. There was no response. Soon, many friends and family members joined in the frantic search for Dawn. Over 10,000 flyers were printed and handed out over two counties. A long-time family friend, Joyce Barrett, came to Mobile and manned the phones, directed traffic, and got a helicopter crew to fly over the area to search for clues.

After 24 hours, the police became involved, officially treating Dawn as a missing person. A Christian police detective was assigned to Dawn's case. On the third day after Dawn's disappearance, a Sunday afternoon, the detective called the family together and said the unthinkable words, "I regret to inform you…" Tears streamed down the detective's face as he told the family that Dawn was dead. He asked the family if he could have the privilege of praying with them and for them. They all joined hands and he prayed a beautiful, powerful prayer that moved their hearts to tears.

Dawn had been abducted from her car in the store parking lot by a 20-year-old man who had been released from Atmore Prison in June. The ex-con forcibly took Dawn to a remote area of Jackson County, Mississippi. There he assaulted her and shot her six times in the face and head. Early Sunday morning, prompted by a guilty conscience and a night of drinking, the killer shot and killed two of his neighbors, then shot a police officer who responded to the resulting emergency call. Numerous police officers were dispatched. The attacker walked out of the house brandishing a high-powered rifle, refusing to put it down. The police were forced to fire on the killer to bring a halt to the deadly situation. Dawn's killer died instantly.

Several months after Dawn's death, Bonnie experienced another astonishing occurrence. Bonnie remembers, "I felt it coming. There was a feeling that I was going to experience something. 'Electric,' maybe, is a good word to describe the encounter." As the strange feelings swirled through Bonnie's heart and mind, the most thrilling, surprising, unexpected thing happened: Bonnie realized her deceased daughter was in the room with her! Dawn gave her mother a hug! Bonnie can still feel the incredible sensation, and tears of joy still threaten as she recalls, "It was so quick that I hardly knew she was there! All she said was 'Mommy. Mommy. Mommy!'"

Many years have passed since Dawn's death. Bonnie says, "Losing a child is devastating; it is like ripping your heart out. When we were told that Dawn was deceased, I knew exactly what was important in this life. I know that God did not kill Dawn. We never blamed God. When evil people do evil things, innocent people are hurt. God cared for us during the ordeal. I believe that God knew our need before we did; He made Himself known to us by the extraordinary experiences to give us strength to get through the ordeal. Losing Dawn has brought some family members closer to Jesus. Not all, but, praise God, some."

Chapter 7

# In the Midst of Faith

In the springtime of 1994, I had been a committed Christian for only three years. I accepted Jesus at the age of ten and received baptism at that time; however, I did not seek the Lord in a committed way. I did not understand the importance of reading the Bible and receiving the Scriptures as spiritual food from Heaven. I did not comprehend the concept and reality of the power of prayer! I did not know it was possible to talk to God; neither did I know it was possible for God to talk to me.

Consequently, I lived most of my life outside the will of God. My conversion to Christianity came in 1991 along with the sincere desire to seek the Lord with all my heart.

*Then you will call upon Me and come and pray to Me, and I will listen to you. You will seek Me and find Me when you search for Me with all your heart* (Jeremiah 29:12-13).

I developed a hunger for reading God's Word.

After only three years, I was still an immature Christian. I experienced trials and tribulations after committing my life to Jesus. That is normal according to the Bible. There had been times when I felt God's presence in ways that simply astounded me. I discovered God can always be found in the midst of enormous trials!

Our daughter, Donna, became very ill only six months after her first son was born. She developed an inflammatory disease that affected her whole body. Donna's physical condition did not improve with time and prayer. She sought medical attention from a physician but he was not helpful. We continued to pray.

March 24, 1994, is a date I cannot forget. That night, I received a message from the Lord in the form of a vision, and I believe God sent the vision to help strengthen our faith. I believe He sent it to help us know how to deal with the illness our daughter faced. It all began as a dream while I was sound asleep. The experience continued as I awoke and sat straight up in bed, wide awake!

> *Indeed God speaks once, or twice, yet no one notices it. In a dream, a vision of the night, when sound sleep falls on men, while they slumber in their beds, then He opens the ears of men, and seals their instruction* (Job 33:14-16).

In the dream, I could see a very old ship with hoisted sails full of wind that caused the sea to lap at the ship's hull with violent waves tossing it back and forth. A heavy anchor beneath the surface held the ship secure. I possessed total comprehension of the ship above and below because I was able to see every portion of the ship as if I had a thousand eyes, positioned above, below, beside, and all around, viewing every inch of the ship's body simultaneously! Trying to remember that particular ability makes my head hurt because that ability is unthinkable and impossible for me as a human. In the vision, God allowed me to experience that ability.

I watched the ship anchored in the storm; it held firm. An invisible hand lifted the anchor and the ship tossed violently, in every direction. When the invisible hand lowered the anchor, the ship rocked but weathered the storm.

When the visual aspect progressed, I heard a genderless monotone voice speaking Scriptures that I recognized immediately from the first chapter of the Book of James. The voice said, *"When you pray, ask in faith, without doubting; to doubt is like a ship being tossed by the waves of the sea."* When the anchor held the ship steady, I comprehended that was faith! When an invisible power raised the anchor, and the ship tossed in uncertainty, I perceived that was doubt!

> *But if any of you lacks wisdom, let him ask of God, who gives to all generously and without reproach, and it will be given to him. But he must ask in faith without any doubting, for the one who doubts is like the surf of the sea, driven and tossed by the wind. For that man ought not to expect that he will receive anything from the Lord, being a double-minded man, unstable in all his ways* (James 1:5-8).

The vision ended when I was sitting up, awake!

I went back to sleep, and the entire vision repeated until I sat wide awake for the second time! I went to sleep again, and the entire vision repeated a third time! As I sat there in bed that third time, I noticed it was five o'clock in the morning. I felt like I had just returned from a trip around the world!

I reached over and gently touched my husband's shoulder, shaking him awake. I did not try to describe the unusual adventure because it was too complex. I simply said, "God is preparing us! Something is coming, and I don't know what. We are going to have to hold onto our faith!"

Within 24 hours, Donna was in the emergency room at Nashville Memorial Hospital. She underwent a series of diagnostic studies and scans. One of the scans revealed a tumor in her left lung. Ever present was the inflammatory process that affected her from the top of her head to the soles of her feet; she suffered greatly!

A pulmonary specialist performed a bronchoscopy in an attempt to get a biopsy of the lung tumor. The doctor was not successful in his attempt because of the location of the tumor. Donna regained consciousness following that procedure then suffered a Vagus spasm. As a result, her pulse disappeared and her heartbeat faded as she lapsed into unconsciousness. The medical team responded quickly, and Donna began breathing normally again in a couple of minutes.

Donna's body was physically drained and emotionally exhausted. Following that frightening episode, she refused further treatment. Her doctor recommended that she have surgery to remove the tumor from the lung; but she refused, saying she would trust God to take care of her. She agreed to go on medication that helped decrease the widespread inflammation and pain.

Against his better judgment, the doctor agreed to abide by her wishes. He suggested she have an X-ray every three months, then every six months to monitor lung changes. I remember the doctor said, "If you live six years, we will know the tumor is not cancer. If you were my daughter, I would insist that you have the surgery at once." She thanked him and declined. I supported her decision because of the vision! I believe God sent the vision to indicate we were to trust Him in the matter, to walk through the affliction by faith.

Many years have passed since that trying time and Donna has lived a normal life since then. So what happened? I can only believe the vision was God's way of conveying to us that life is survivable when we walk by faith. It was a time of testing!

> *Beloved, do not be surprised at the fiery ordeal among you, which comes upon you for your testing, as though some strange thing were happening to you* (1 Peter 4:12).

The repetition of the vision led me to believe Donna's illness would be prolonged, that unwavering faith would be required in order to endure it. Donna was not healed in an instant. She was healed over a prolonged period of time. God granted her the ability to live in spite of her physical affliction. *I do not recommend the route Donna chose to anyone who reads this!* Each individual should respond based on his or her own particular circumstances.

Through the years and the trials, I have discovered that life is never easy. We survive the trials with God's help. He is with us in the good times and the bad times.

*...The Lord is my helper, I will not be afraid...* (Hebrews 13:6).

# Chapter 8

# His Ways

God made the heavens, the earth, and the universe. I have no doubt that He spoke light and darkness into existence and created the sun, moon, and stars. It is easy for me to accept the awesome might and power of God with the faith of a child.

However, I suppose the ways of the Lord in the details of life will seem foreign to me as long as I am on this side of Heaven. His concern over the minutiae of life will always amaze and delight me. Why would Almighty God bother Himself with the seemingly trivial or insignificant things—little things, such as an earring?

My husband and I prepared to leave town early one morning. The car was packed, and I had just fastened the clasp on my wristwatch and put on my earrings. I turned to walk out of the bedroom and I heard a quiet voice say, "Go, and look in the mirror." I paused for a moment questioning why I should receive such instruction, then did as the voice had directed me. I turned on the light and looked closely at myself in the mirror. Then I saw it! One earring was an ordinary white pearl and the other was a silver ball.

With a smile and a bit of wonder I said, "Thank You, Lord."

Would it have mattered if I had worn mismatched earrings? Certainly not. I would have been annoyed by the mistake, but it really would not have mattered in the end. But for some reason, it mattered to the Lord.

That kind of divine intervention is puzzling to me. I am so thankful that God notices everything! I just do not know why He bothers. The fact remains that He does; and I love Him for looking after me.

I remember one summer when everyone in my family had too much going on in their lives. They were always gone from home and I ended up cutting the grass until late one evening. The house was empty and quiet when I finished working in the yard and headed in for a shower. Just as I entered the bedroom, I heard a voice say, "Kneel and pray." I received no instruction as to what I should pray, but I obeyed. I stepped toward the side of the bed and dropped to my knees. I prayed and thanked God for our blessings. I remained there a moment just waiting for further direction, but I heard nothing else.

As I arose from my kneeling position, I turned my head to the left and looked toward the floor. A huge spider scurried off the leg of my jeans and onto the carpet. I killed the spider with my shoe! I remember thanking God for showing me the spider before it bit me or got under the bed! He knew my aversion to spiders, and once again, He was watching over me.

One more story!

One morning, after working in the flower bed on the side of our home, I was alone in the house and walking though the upstairs hall. A voice distinctly said, "Look out the window." I walked to the nearest window and looked out over the flower bed. I admired the freshly cut grass and the shade provided by the two tall hickory trees in the yard; but I was puzzled by that long, straight, black stick near the flower bed. I was sure I had cleaned up all the debris around the flower bed, and the stick should not have been there. At that moment, the long, black stick began to crawl and slither from side to side until it ended up in the flower bed! It was a very long, blacksnake. I detest snakes and avoid them with great care. When my husband returned home, he searched until he found the snake, then he carried it off by the tail. The snake wasn't poisonous, but it *was* still a snake. Once again, the Lord protected me!

Why would anyone ever doubt God about anything? He is all-powerful, full of love and forgiveness, and He is in charge. He keeps up with the entire universe and still manages to let me know when I am wearing mismatched earrings and warns me about spiders and snakes. He knows the exact number of hairs on my head and knows when a sparrow (or spider) falls.

> *"For My thoughts are not your thoughts, nor are your ways My ways," declares the Lord. "For as the heavens are higher than the earth, so are My ways higher than your ways, and My thoughts than your thoughts"* (Isaiah 55:8-9).

Chapter 9

# I Am Coming to See You

Brenda Doster, a Baptist minister's wife, possessed a generous heart and a sincere desire to serve and love others. She lived in Dresden, Tennessee; she spent much of her time living simply and working with her hands. She lived her faith and was known for her laughter and singing. Brenda was a talented piano player. Brenda's daughter, Deanna, grew up thinking all moms cooked delicious food, kept spotless homes, painted walls, and fixed electrical problems as her mom did!

When continuous leg pain crept into Brenda's life, she initially treated it as a nuisance. The pain persisted and increased in severity until Brenda sought medical attention. In the summer of 2006, Brenda learned she had a large tumor in her leg as well as a mass in her abdomen. A surgeon removed the tumors, and Brenda began her arduous journey with colon cancer. Doctors encouraged her to have chemotherapy. One doctor told her, "If you take the treatment, you may live. If you do not take the treatment, you will die."

Reluctantly, Brenda agreed to the treatment; however, it did not cure the cancer. It made her symptoms worse. Brenda became weak and disoriented. The winter passed and springtime emerged, bringing forth dogwood blossoms, daffodils—and hope! Brenda's faith did not fail her and she struggled to survive the deadly assault on her body. She completed the chemo treatments in early April.

In spite of a courageous battle, the aggressive disease spread to other organs in Brenda's weakened body. She left the hospital and opted to spend her last days at home under hospice care. Brenda became bed-ridden and incapacitated by severe pain. The cancer, coupled with strong pain medication, cause Brenda to slip into a semi-conscious state. Her words became few and when she spoke, her voice was only a whisper.

With only days to live, Brenda surprised her caregivers and family one day. Brenda startled her daughter, Deanna, when she sat up and called out in an unusually strong and stern voice. Brenda sat up with wide eyes, exclaiming repeatedly, "Sit me up, sit me up!"

Brenda focused her eyes on something incredible and supernatural! She gazed ahead and slightly upward, clearly conversing with her deceased mother and Jesus! She smiled and waved her hand to them, saying, "I am coming to see you, I am coming to see you!" She was overjoyed and caught up in a heavenly experience over which she had no control.

David Freeman, a Baptist minister and Deanna's husband, entered the room as soon as his wife called out to him. David said, "When I walked into the room, I noticed Brenda's eyes were wide open, yet she looked through me. I was told that just prior to my arrival she spoke directly to her mother and Jesus as if they were visible, yet some distance away. Brenda seemed to be looking through a heavenly window! She appeared to communicate with those not of this realm with ease and she apparently saw a magnificent and glorious scene!"

"Suddenly, she became very excited and with a smile on her face, Brenda began clapping her hands in appreciation of what was on display before her! Her actions reminded me of a child watching fireworks for the first time. She was filled with joy and amazement! She cried out, 'Thank You Jesus, thank You Jesus!' She repeated that phrase over and over again for over a minute, all the while clapping and raising her hands, even at one point letting out an old fashioned shout to the Lord," said David.

David continued, "As I reflect on that day, the words of Romans 8:18 come to mind. *'For I consider that the sufferings of this present time are not worthy to be compared with the glory that is to be revealed to us.'* In that moment, the cancer that seemed so powerful and menacing just moments before seemed insignificant in the light of the Glory that was being revealed. Having witnessed that event, I am more convinced now than ever before that Heaven is real! One day all Christians will find themselves overwhelmed as they see Jesus in all His glory. No matter what we suffer in the meantime, it will simply fade away in the light of Christ! Standing at the foot of that bed, I longed for Heaven like I have never done before!"

Brenda Doster died two days later at the age of 58. Her hope of being healed on earth and traveling to many churches to share her miraculous healing did not come to pass. Perhaps Brenda's dying testimony will encourage others in a significant way to seek Jesus first and foremost. Her heavenly experience encourages me not to despair under the weight of life's sufferings. A better home surely awaits us if we belong to Christ!

> *The city* [heaven] *is laid out as a square, and its length is as great as the width...fifteen hundred miles; its length and width and height are equal.... The material of the wall was jasper; and the city was pure gold, like clear glass. ...And the city has no need of the sun or of the moon to shine on it, for the glory of God has illumined it, and its lamp is the Lamb* [Jesus].*...Nothing unclean, and no one who practices abomination and lying, shall ever come into it, but only those whose names are written in the Lamb's book of life* (Revelation 21:16,18,23,27).

Chapter 10

# Realities

Bart Bell's sport was tandem racing, a cycling competition in which the contestants ride bicycles built for two. However, racing tandems are far different from the recreational cycles with which most are familiar; these tandems are not equipped with brakes and they are built for speed. Propelled by two highly trained athletes, in the final lap of tandem races these mechanical marvels can reach speeds of nearly 50 miles per hour!

Bart's preferred event was the tandem sprint, a race of a little over a mile (1.66 kilometers) held in a stadium called a velodrome. The velodrome contains a 333-meter track with banked curves. The slope at either end of the velodrome track rises at an incredible 180 degrees. During a race, each tandem cycle is manned by a pilot (or captain) who steers and sets the pace, and a co-pilot (or stoker) who works in conjunction with the pilot. The two must think and act as one during these exciting and dangerous competitions. High speeds and no brakes guarantee an interesting race and an unpredictable finish!

In 1992, Bart Bell was living in San Diego, California. He had spent years perfecting his sport, the last eight in actual tandem sprint competition. At the age of 24, it appeared his dream was about to come true— Bart was now an Olympian hopeful. The final race for this Olympic World Championship finalist took place in Blaine, Minnesota. The results would determine whether Bart would go to the Olympics in Barcelona, Spain, as the tandem sprint pilot or would be held in reserve as the backup captain.

On June 28, 1992, the race took place as planned. Everything was going well; Bart and teammate Tom Brinker were burning up the track at approximately 45 miles per hour when the unthinkable happened. Bart and Tom were thrown from their cycle by a mid-sprint collision.

Bart received a broken nose and suffered a severe, closed-head injury that left him comatose for two weeks. He regained consciousness, but weeks passed before Bart's cognitive ability was fully restored. More than five weeks after the accident, Bart experienced his first moment of clarity when he saw the Olympic ceremonies on television. His first thought was, "I'm supposed to be there. I must have overslept!"

His cuts and scrapes healed, but Bart suffered physical deficits caused by the head injury. He was extremely lethargic, sleeping most days for 18 to 20 hours. The left side of his body was paralyzed and the head injuries left him with short-term amnesia. Bart could remember being five years old; he could recall his phone number from when he was seven; but Bart had no memory of the crash or the days immediately surrounding it. Oddly, he felt young, like a small child. It was as though his brain had taken him to a safe place to recuperate.

During his first conscious moments, Bart was aware something unusual had happened. He felt changed; something about him was different beyond the physical injuries. Bart remembers: "I knew something. I didn't know *what* I knew, but something was different in my soul, in my heart, in my being. I didn't talk about it; I just thought about it. In the days that followed, it became clearer in my head and in my heart what actually transpired."

Slowly, Bart's memory of the events he experienced while comatose returned. They became clearer as the days progressed. Bart remembers lying with his toes pointing up, as the hands of a clock would point to twelve; however, his feet seemed to be pointing toward 11.

"I was at the gates of Heaven," Bart recalls. "I was not inside the gates. There was a male voice, which I didn't recognize, and the voice said, 'Don't look at the light.' A bright, white light was shining from behind my right shoulder. I did not look at the light."

The experience continued as he remained flat on his back looking at his toes. Soon, Bart's deceased grandmother walked up and stood near his feet. Her voice was distinct and familiar. She told him, "You're not going to stay; you're going back." Then, Carl Leusenkamp, Bart's coach who had died in 1990, appeared next to Bart's grandmother and imparted the same message: "You're not going to stay; you're going back." Bart's grandmother and his coach continued speaking to Bart to encourage him, reassuring him he would be all right.

"After their visits, I had no feelings of insecurity, anxiety, or hopelessness, only positive feelings," Bart remembers. "I'm not sure if they spoke words with their mouths, but I'm sure they spoke with love. I do know that I heard their words distinctly in their own familiar voices."

Bart struggled to describe the feelings he experienced during the strange encounter. "It's like trying to describe a roller coaster ride. As you describe it, you can feel it. I have said many times, I don't have the words in my vocabulary to describe the awesomeness of what happened to me. I don't know those words. It's beyond my vocabulary to speak of it. All I can do is make analogies. I could feel, I could taste, I could hear, I could smell; I was using all my senses, and I could feel the love. The love was alive. It was a light blue mist. There was love all around me. It was just there. I don't know where it came from or where it went. It was just there; and it was overwhelming. I was experiencing love through all my senses, and I was actually breathing in love."

As Bart's consciousness returned, he was filled with a "knowing." The love he experienced remained and seemed to permeate his entire being. He felt exhilaration! He had no way of knowing if this near-death experience took place at the moment of the collision or at some point during the coma.

"I don't speak of this often," Bart explains, "but when I do, I get the same exhilaration in my heart that I felt while I was there. My dad was the first one I talked with about what happened. I told him, 'Something's different, something happened.' There is more going on than our five senses can perceive. It is around us and in us. It's not scary, but it *is* overwhelming!"

Bart endured a long and difficult period of recovery and rehabilitation. With courage and determination, he recovered from his injuries and walks today with a mild limp. The Lord took Bart on a heavenly journey and Bart clearly received His message. He began to understand his earthly journey was really just beginning. Bart could now face his future with a new and profound understanding!

It has been many years since Bart's accident. He now owns his own successful business and lives in Colorado Springs, Colorado, with his wife, Carri, and their four children. Though that fateful collision ended his Olympic dreams, God left Bart with a winning spirit in his heart and the ability to fulfill his destiny. He views his near-death experience as a gift from God to help him live his life by faith. He wakes up at 5:30 each morning looking for the adventure life has to offer. Bart expectantly meets each day asking of God, "What do I do today? What's next? Where do I go from here?"

Today, when Bart stops to consider the incredible experiences he has lived, his present circumstances, and the full comprehension of the place where he will spend eternity, he responds with heartfelt enthusiasm: "I'm just so blessed and thankful! It's wonderful to be alive!"

# Chapter 11

# A Desperate Plea

Cold rain fell on that dark winter evening as the temperature plummeted to 14 degrees. My husband and I felt uneasy when we realized the roads were becoming very slippery. We lived in the country near Mt. Juliet, Tennessee. Our home was quite a ways from downtown Nashville where our son David was attending a night class at Belmont University.

David left the campus at eight o'clock that evening. He drove a new black Mustang, the car of his dreams! It was still an unfamiliar car to him and lightweight. Mustangs were not designed for traveling over icy roads. David had never attempted to drive on ice before; we knew he might be in for some trouble.

Our son began his trip home traveling east on Interstate 40. In a matter of minutes, he realized the Mustang was no match for the present road conditions. I felt helpless each time he called with a progress report. The frozen roads were so treacherous that many cars could not even make it off the exit ramps. David had no choice but to continue eastward. He tried to console me by reminding me what I already knew, "Mom, the Lord is with me!" I knew he was right.

My husband and I prayed together and asked God to send angels to protect David. We prayed for all the motorists who were out that night. Suddenly, I felt the urge to talk to God alone. I went into our bedroom and closed the door. I prayed, "Lord, You can do anything! Will You just melt the ice before him and bring David home safely tonight, please?"

When I arose, the fear was gone, and I had a certain knowledge that David should detour from his planned route. I had an inner peace that he should make his way toward Andrew Jackson Parkway! It was unlikely that road would be salted, but I knew what God imparted when I prayed.

David agreed to change his course as soon as he was able and I felt a sense of relief! From that moment on, Burke and I knew what we needed to do. We prepared the four-wheel-drive SUV for any foreseeable difficulties we might encounter and drove toward David with great caution. We saw many cars in ditches, yet we moved slowly but surely along at a snail's pace.

We were pleasantly surprised when our son called to say he had managed to reach the hardware store in Hermitage. He said, "This is as far as I go! My car is in one piece, and I am going to park it here!"

When we arrived, David was happy to see us! The first thing he said was, "Man oh man! What a trip! I was glad to see the ice melted on Andrew Jackson Parkway! I was the only car in sight, and I drove at normal speed. Water sprayed up from my tires as I drove!"

We traveled home the same way we came, very slowly and on ice. We all knew it was not possible for ice to melt when the temperature was 14 degrees. It was not humanly possible for our son to drive at normal speed with water splashing on the side of his car! That night, we received a reminder… *"With God all things are possible"* (Matt. 19:26).

I believe a merciful heavenly Father heard a desperate mother's childlike plea for her faithful son. He answered her prayer by sending just what she asked for and God received the glory. God still receives the glory today each time the story is told!

The situation required assistance that only God could provide! Our family made it home safely and we arrived in our warm, country kitchen where the embers glowed in the fireplace, inviting us to warm our cold hands. It was so good to be home; our family was safe and under one roof! God's divine intervention demonstrated His real presence. Prayers of praise and thanksgiving overflowed from our hearts as we drifted off to sleep with the assurance that we were surely loved and safe in our heavenly Father's care.

> *He* [God] *sends forth His command to the earth; His word runs very swiftly. He gives snow like wool; He scatters the frost like ashes. He casts forth His ice as fragments; who can stand before His cold? He sends forth His word and melts them* [the ice]; *He causes His wind to blow and the waters to flow* (Psalm 147:15-18).

Chapter 12

# Voice of a Friend

S ummer was Annie Scheele's favorite time of year. The Atlantic shore beckoned, and Annie often took her daughter, Leila, to enjoy the golden warmth of the beach near their Rockville, Maryland, home. Annie was thrilled each time she watched three-year-old Leila's eyes light up with excitement as they walked across the beautiful expanse of sparkling sand to the water's edge.

Louis, the 17-year-old brother of Annie's childhood friend, often joined Annie and Leila on the beach that summer. Louis and Leila had formed a grand friendship. They took long walks together, waves lapping at their feet as they searched for seashells to add to Leila's growing collection. Leila adored Louis, and he seemed to enjoy his time with the little girl. He became a welcome addition to their beach outings. Louis was an all-around good kid.

Annie was sure the summer of 1977 was one she would long remember.

Several months later, the bitter winds of winter descended. One particularly cold December night, Louis left a party and sat in his car as the engine idled. Unaware of the deadly carbon monoxide fumes that seeped into the vehicle, Louis soon lost consciousness. Louis' young life was cut short; he died that frozen, winter night from accidental carbon monoxide poisoning. His premature death was a tragic ending to a life that offered so much promise.

A short time after Louis died, Leila rode in the back seat of the car as Annie navigated heavy traffic on Piercefield Road. Annie's day had been stressful and she was not nearly as focused on driving as she should have been. With her mind on other matters, Annie was oblivious to the congested intersection just ahead of her. Suddenly, she felt a strong hand grab her shoulder and she clearly heard Louis yell, "Annie, red light!" Without hesitation, she responded to the voice; she hit the brakes, bringing the car to a sudden stop just short of the busy intersection. An inevitable accident had been avoided. Had she not stopped when she did, she and Leila could have been severely injured, maybe even killed.

Thoughts raced through Annie's mind! From the back seat, Leila said, "Mommy, Louis is with us, and he told you to stop, didn't he?" It was a profound moment. Louis was certainly dead. Yet, Annie could still feel his hand as he grabbed her shoulder; she could still hear his voice as he yelled the warning that saved their lives. Louis had been with them in the car, and she and Leila both heard him!

Annie cannot explain her after-death encounter with Louis; but she firmly believes no explanation is necessary. Her faith was challenged, encouraged, and strengthened by the experience; and she has gained a certain and sure peace. Annie says she is keenly aware that the body is just a shell for something much greater than this temporary life; it is the container for the eternal soul.

Though the events may be beyond rationalization, Annie remains convinced that something miraculous and incredible occurred that day on Piercefield Road.

# Chapter 13

# Pray!

In the winter of 1996, something unusual happened every day for two weeks. I awoke at four o'clock each morning and each time, I was strongly compelled to pray. Some mornings, I was startled awake. Other mornings, I felt a hand on my shoulder, gently shaking me. It was not a human hand! Each time I climbed out of bed and obeyed the voice that was silent to my ears yet audible to my spirit.

My family and I lived in a wonderful, rambling farmhouse surrounded by 47 acres of trees and Tennessee wildlife. My husband and I claimed the downstairs part of the house while our son David laid claim to half of the upstairs area. That left half of the upstairs area for our daughter, her husband, and their son. Our son-in-law was still in college, so we encouraged them to share our home. We had more than enough space. During that time, we were three generations under one roof, and I will always cherish the memories of that precious era that has long since passed.

My pre-dawn prayer place was in the middle of the family room downstairs. When I began seeking the Lord at four o'clock each morning, I routinely lit a large candle in the center of the coffee table and knelt there. The early morning wake-up calls continued for a period of two weeks. The Lord did not tell me why I was to spend extra time with Him; He just imparted to me that I should pray, and I obeyed.

One evening, I was standing at the sink washing the supper dishes when our son David came home from a night class at Belmont University.

I looked over my shoulder at him, smiled, and said, "I'm glad you're home!" He had a perplexed look on his face and his hand rested on his upper chest.

David said, "Something is wrong," indicating something was wrong in his upper chest area. Because David never complained, I knew he was experiencing a real problem. The look on his face, the sound of his voice, and the way he held his chest sent chills over me. I sensed a dark presence and the hair on the back of my neck literally stood up. The Bible tells us that satan is the thief who comes only to steal, kill, and destroy! I quieted the intruder by speaking the last part of that Scripture that says Jesus came so that we might have life and have it abundantly! (See John 10:10.)

In my spirit, I heard the Lord saying, "This is why I wanted you to pray more than usual for the past two weeks. Your faith must be strong!" I tried not to sound alarmed as I told David I would call our doctor in the morning and ask him to do an examination.

Dr. Seeley saw David the next day and scheduled a diagnostic study at Tennessee Medical Center in Madison, Tennessee, for the following day. David went straight from Belmont to the hospital for the test shortly after lunch time.

I remember going through my day as usual when I was overwhelmed with the feeling that I really needed to go to the hospital. I dropped everything and drove to the hospital.

The diagnostic study took a very long time when it should have taken no more than 30 minutes. When David appeared in the waiting room, he appeared unsettled. I asked the nurse if the test showed any abnormality, and she searched for the right words. She said, "You will have to talk with your doctor on Monday." I questioned persistently, and the radiologist agreed to speak to me. He said the test showed a very large esophageal tumor. I thanked him, and we left the hospital and headed home.

Before I reached our home, Dr. Seeley called and said he had scheduled an appointment on Monday for David to see a gastroenterologist. He expressed the seriousness and the urgency of the situation. I thanked him and attempted to gather my wits so I could be in a good frame of mind when I got home.

Over the weekend, my husband and I prayed without ceasing, and I meditated on the Scriptures, especially the ones that promised God would heal if we only believe! I watched from the window as David pitched a ball to Jacob, our little grandson. The football ended up on top of the roof above the patio. David attempted to retrieve the ball by climbing out a second story window. I helped him remove the screen. I touched his back as he crawled back through the window and, somehow, I knew at that moment God had healed David! I truly believed, but I needed confirmation.

On Monday I accompanied David to the pre-arranged appointment with the gastroenterologist, and we listened as the doctor gave his opinion based on the esophagram results and the radiologist report. He advised us there was a chance the tumor would be malignant. He suggested a biopsy right away and advised us to have the operation done at Vanderbilt Medical Center in Nashville. Dr. Winters said the surgery would alter David's life drastically. A section of the esophagus would be removed. This would necessitate pulling the upper stomach up to close the gap. A lifetime of medication and a special diet would follow. That was the good news. If it was cancer and if it had spread, those procedures would not help at all.

My brain tried to digest what the doctor said, but my spirit said I should have no part of what he was saying! I asked him to schedule the biopsy for Friday, knowing that would give us a week to seek the Lord and wait for His guidance. I was aware of what the Bible taught us. *"Do not fear, for I am with you"* (Isaiah 41:10).

David was young, and I loved him so much! I could not bear the thought of an unnecessary surgical procedure. I prayed, saying, "Lord,

I asked You to heal David completely, causing the tumor to wither and cease to exist, and I believe You have healed him!" The room was still dark, but I saw the face of a man before my eyes! The face disappeared in a few seconds. The face was hazy but I thought, *I must know him!* I said, "Lord, that face looked like Dr. Fox." I saw nothing else. I thought, *"This doctor will give us confirmation that the tumor is gone!"*

Dr. Fox was a physician I met on one occasion in the past. I recalled he was a medical missionary earlier in his life. I searched the phone book and located his number. I called and talked with his office manager. I briefly explained our situation and I told her, "I know my son has been healed. Please see if Dr. Fox will examine him." Later that same day, David and I sat in Dr. Fox's office. I briefly explained our situation and my firm belief that God had healed David on Saturday. Dr. Fox understood, and he agreed to order a CT scan, which would confirm or deny that the healing had taken place.

Dr. Fox called Thursday morning with wonderful news! He said, "The CT scan revealed there is no tumor. It showed only a calcified, withered lymph node where the tumor was shown on the previous study." I was elated! God had healed our son! Dr. Fox even used the word "withered." That was the same word I had used when I prayed, asking God to cause the tumor to wither and cease to exist. I knew we had confirmation from God, letting us know He had heard our prayers and He had answered our prayers!

We canceled the Friday biopsy appointment. Our family engaged in a faith walk of prayer and believing. God required us to seek His face. We had to listen with a sensitive and obedient spirit, then follow through on what God showed us. We had to trust God and proceed a little at a time. That is how God works!

We thanked the Lord, and we gave Him the glory for healing David and teaching us to trust Him no matter what. God's divine intervention gave David the gift of life that day. May we never forget! Our Lord, once again, had shown us compassion, mercy, and love.

# Chapter 14

# Foretold

Glenda Raines* was only 32 years old when she began to have severe, incapacitating headaches. Her family physician had referred her to a neurosurgeon, Dr. Arthur Cushman, in Nashville. When she arrived in his office for her first appointment, she was awake and fully coherent; however, she was very drowsy.

Dr. Cushman sent Glenda directly to the intensive care unit of Nashville Memorial Hospital. Tests were immediately performed, and it was discovered Glenda had elevated intracranial pressure. Dr. Cushman started her on high doses of steroids to lower the pressure in her brain. Further studies revealed Glenda was suffering the effects of a malignant brain tumor.

Dr. Cushman met with Glenda late that same day and gently informed her of his diagnosis. He told her he would perform the surgery to remove the cancerous growth; it was scheduled for the next day.

At first, Glenda's reaction seemed typical as she absorbed the frightening news—Glenda expressed a certainty that she would die during the surgery. Many patients facing life-threatening surgery are fearful and speak of impending death, so Dr. Cushman was not overly concerned about Glenda's prediction and offered words of comfort and encouragement. However, Glenda persisted, seemingly convinced she had foreseen the coming events that would end in her death.

On the day of her surgery, Dr. Cushman visited Glenda early during morning rounds. Glenda spoke plainly to him of the premonition she had suggested the night before, "Dr. Cushman, I know I am going to die today during the surgery."

Again, the doctor tried to assure her that her fears were normal considering the situation. But Glenda seemed strangely reconciled and at peace with the fate she predicted. She proceeded to tell the doctor precise details of what she believed would take place during the surgery: who would be present, what would be said, where Dr. Cushman would be standing, and the specific events preceding her inevitable death. Dr. Cushman tried to project a confident, reassuring attitude, but he felt extremely uneasy in the face of Glenda's certainty. Glenda was convinced death awaited her inside the operating room.

Later in the day, Dr. Cushman was performing a craniotomy on another patient when he received a frantic call from the intensive care unit. The nurse quickly relayed the facts of Glenda's worsening condition, "She is unconscious. She has nearly stopped breathing. Both of her pupils are fixed and dilated."

Dr. Cushman knew Glenda's condition was critical; she was fighting for her life. Dr. Cushman realized there was no time to lose. "Give the patient Mannitol (a drug that rapidly shrinks the brain), put in a breathing tube, shave her head, and send her to the operating room at once!"

Nurses moved quickly to prepare the adjacent operating room for an emergency craniotomy. No other neurosurgeons were available that day, leaving Dr. Cushman no choice but to stop the first surgery and operate on Glenda.

When Dr. Cushman opened Glenda's skull, he discovered she had developed a massive hemorrhage. There was nothing Dr. Cushman could do to stop the appalling loss of blood. Glenda died on the operating table within minutes of the discovery.

Dr. Cushman was seriously shaken; the series of events had occurred exactly as Glenda had predicted. Vision or premonition, call it what you like, but Glenda had somehow already observed the final moments of her life on earth; she had watched herself die. She had been 100 percent correct in her prophecy, down to the last detail!

Dr. Cushman met with Glenda's family and candidly explained what had happened. Amazingly, the family members appeared to be at peace when they received the news. They told Dr. Cushman that Glenda had forewarned them of her impending death. Though they were saddened by grief, Glenda had enabled them to prepare themselves for the inevitable.

Dazed by the events of the day, Dr. Cushman returned to the surgery that had been interrupted. The surgery ended successfully, but Dr. Cushman knew he had experienced a day he would never forget.

*The fictitious name Glenda Raines was used to protect the identity of Dr. Cushman's deceased patient.*

## Chapter 15

# Pray for Rain!

It was wintertime when I became ill and could not seem to shake the aches and pains and recurring headaches. I exercised, ate right, and took vitamins, but did not feel better as I expected. I did not want to see the doctor, so I prayed and believed I would get well.

I had been a believer for five years at the time, and I was still somewhat confused when it came to God's will for healing. I knew He healed some people some of the time but not all of the people all of the time. I really believed if I prayed for healing, I should not see a doctor because taking that action would indicate a lack of faith.

One day, I was doing housework and putting out clean towels. As I worked quietly, I asked the Lord to help me understand about healing, and I asked Him to clear up my uncertainty. As quickly as the thought left my brain, the Lord spoke to my spirit, saying, *"If your foot is on fire, it is not wrong to pour a bucket of water on it. It is right to pray for rain!"*

My mouth dropped open because I was surprised that He responded so quickly and a little shocked about the manner in which He spoke! I had to think about what He said. His response was very different from the way I had heard Him before. His reply was very interesting. I smiled in amazement.

I continued my housework, trying to decipher His remark. I arrived at the conclusion that faith begins where our ability ends! When we are out of human solutions, then God provides His holy solution! If aspirin can relieve the pain temporarily and my faith is not strong enough to believe for complete healing, then I should use the aspirin. I assumed the phrase "pray for rain" meant I should pray for stronger faith to believe God for a permanent cure. After all, we can only receive what we are able to believe we can receive. *Faith defies logic!*

I found it interesting that day that God would use the foot in an analogy about healing. It is equally interesting that in the Book of Matthew, when Jesus walked on the earth, He spoke of the foot in an analogy about stumbling blocks. In both cases, the Lord spoke matter of factly when making His point clearly.

> *If your hand or your foot causes you to stumble, cut it off and throw it from you; it is better for you to enter life crippled or lame, than to have two hands or two feet and be cast into the eternal fire. If your eye causes you to stumble, pluck it out and throw it from you. It is better for you to enter life with one eye, than to have two eyes and be cast into the fiery hell* (Matthew 18:8-9).

# Chapter 16

# No Fear

Jacqueline Elkins, a former nurse and clinic manager, was going through a very difficult time in her life. Her husband had recently walked away from her and ended their marriage, leaving Jacque feeling rejected, confused, and alone. Her faith was severely tested and shaken by the recent deaths of her father and sister. It was all too much; Jacque's heart was bruised and broken.

The second day of May was a beautiful, blue-sky day. Now on her own, Jacque decided to tackle the unfamiliar task of trimming the shrubs in her yard. She borrowed a hedge trimmer and an extension cord from her son-in-law who lived across the street. Jacque connected the extension cord to the trimmer plug and tossed the cord across her shoulder to avoid cutting it.

As she trimmed the shrub from the bottom upward, the trimmer plug and cord outlet separated slightly, allowing her necklace chain to fall into the crack. The chain acted as a perfect conductor for the electricity. As her gold cross pendant melted and the bone-jarring currents coursed through Jacque's body, the realization hit—she was being electrocuted!

Jacque remained vertical as the electrical current caused the muscles throughout her body to convulse and her heart rhythm to falter. Her eyeballs felt like they were being wrenched from their sockets. Searing pain resulted from a rupture in her right breast where the electricity exited her body. Sounds made by passing cars, the lawn mower next door, and the laughter of children down the street remained constant—her senses remained intact.

Suddenly, Jacque realized, "I'm about to meet God!" At that point, an overwhelming sense of peace filled Jacque. The following account is in Jacque's own words.

"I cannot describe the peace that I felt. All fear left me; I had no regrets or anxious thoughts. There was only peace. I looked up into that lovely blue sky, and I saw one billowy, cumulous-looking cloud. The distance between the cloud and me was closing in. I could not tell if the cloud was descending toward me or if I was ascending toward the cloud! The cloud was three dimensional. The part of the cloud that extended closest to me was the purest white I had ever seen. Shades of dark blue, unlike the blue-sky background, rimmed the cloud and resembled a transparent blue mist. Knowledge was imparted to me, allowing me to comprehend that Jesus was in the cloud coming for me. I was dying and Jesus gave me the intellectual capacity to know that. I was not afraid."

The thought, *Jesus, remove this cord from me,* passed through Jacque's brain. Before the thought was completed, the cord fell from Jacque's body! She immediately fell to the ground, engulfed in a personal inferno. Jacque was on fire! The skin on her neck and torso were swallowed by the flames.

When she was finally able to make a sound, Jacque screamed. Her son-in-law, Jim, heard and ran to her aid. The flames were leaping above Jacque's head! Jim managed to pull the burning shirt away from her severely burned body.

Jacque remained conscious as the ambulance sped toward the burn center at Vanderbilt Medical Center in Nashville, Tennessee. Though racked by intense pain, she told the doctor in the emergency room about the cloud she saw as she looked up at the sky. The doctor responded by saying, "When you are being electrocuted, you have no voluntary muscle control. It would have been impossible for you to tilt your head back to look up. You were seeing up through your spirit's eyes. You were at the point of death."

Jacque's heart began to change. In the midst of the emergency room chaos, Jacque became keenly aware she no longer feared death. She realized the grief she felt over the deaths of her father and sister had miraculously been replaced by a sense of knowing they were all right. Jacque knew, beyond a shadow of doubt, she had been in the presence of Jesus and had been changed by her near-death experience. It seemed all the Scriptures she ever read came to life within her. The words of Second Corinthians 5:8 echoed in her head and reverberated in her heart, *"We are of good courage, I say, and prefer rather to be absent from the body and to be at home with the Lord."*

The intensive care unit became Jacque's home for the next three days as the doctors stabilized her condition. Morphine dulled her pain; however, she remained cognizant of her situation and everything that was going on around her.

Jacque remembers, "I never felt alone. A huge man, who appeared to be eight feet tall, sat in a chair at the side of my bed. His shoulders, arms, and hands were large and muscular. The man's medium-length, brown, wavy hair touched his shoulders. He wore khaki-colored clothing. He never looked at me. He watched the door intently. I innately knew he was a protector—an angel sent by God to keep satan from entering my room. I knew satan wanted me dead, but God wanted me alive." No one who visited Jackie was able to see the angel, but Jacque observed him for the entire three days of her stay in intensive care.

> *The thief comes only to steal and kill and destroy; I came that they may have life, and have it abundantly* (John 10:10).

The truth of this Scripture was firmly embedded in Jacque's heart and mind.

Jacque's initial treatment resulted in a hospital stay of several weeks. During this time, Jacque endured numerous skin grafts and suffered from complications caused by scar tissue.

Even after her release, she was plagued by residual problems. As the damaged nerves began to regenerate, Jacque suffered relentless, intolerable pain. A buildup of fibrous, inflexible scar tissue resulted in Jacque's inability to turn her head from side to side. Physicians were unable to alleviate the life-altering conditions with which Jacque was forced to live each day. The pain was ruthless and her suffering constant.

Jacque attended a church healing service. A minister laid hands on her and prayed for healing. The changes in Jacque's condition were immediately evident as her excruciating pain subsided, and the scar tissue became more pliant, allowing her to turn her head. God's miraculous healing power amazed Jackie!

Over the following decade, Jacque endured numerous life-threatening physical conditions; however, God always sustained her. Jacque remains convinced that divine intervention spared her life and provided the opportunity for her to share with others her near-death experience and incredible message of hope!

# Chapter 17

# The Vision

The summer of 1997 was an unforgettable one. June started out joyfully; however, it ended very sadly. Two families who were dear to our hearts each lost a child that June. Baby girl Haley Little died from an infection, and young J.J. Edwards died in a freak accident involving a train and tractor collision. The deaths brought back memories. A few years back, my sister and her husband lost their precious little Ashley when she drowned in a backyard pool. When there is death, there is always the pain of letting go. Each tragedy reminded us that children are the hardest ones to let go.

On a Saturday afternoon the last week of June, my body was physically and emotionally drained. My words of encouragement spoken to grieving family members sounded as cold and empty as an echo in a canyon. How I wished I could ease some of the pain in the broken hearts of those people who had suffered such great loss. The loss and separation was so new that nothing could help them except the Lord. My heart ached for them!

The afternoon was drawing to a close when I retreated to a quiet room and closed the door. I needed to be alone with God to pray for those people. I lifted up each person along with their loss and prayed for relief from the suffering they were experiencing.

I remember saying, "Lord, You can do anything! You can just touch them with the tip of Your finger and make them better. Please do something for them! Father, won't You give them something to ease the pain and make them better." Honestly, I was not expecting an audible reply from the Lord. I was confused when I received such a reply! Immediately the Lord spoke firmly, saying, "You give them something."

I was silent. I didn't know how to respond. After a respectful pause, I said, "Lord, I don't have anything to give them."

A disturbing vision was revealed to me at that time. I saw an exhibition before me that resembled a scene on a movie screen. There was an endless sea of faces all wearing theatrical masks with downturned mouths and downturned eyes. They were crying out loudly, and their arms reached toward Heaven. The outcry of grief was deafening and heartbreaking emotionally. The faces vanished from sight as suddenly as they appeared.

These words came next, *"If you extract the precious from the worthless, you will become My spokesman."* I recognized the Scripture from the Book of Jeremiah and later searched for the address. It was Jeremiah 15:19.

There in the stillness and quiet, I heard a song in my head. The lyrics and melody came at the same time. I captured the song on paper and mentally noted the melody. I remained quiet for several minutes but neither saw nor heard anything after that.

The feelings I had during those few minutes were unshakable in the days that followed. I realized I had heard from God but did not know what to make of it. Days later, I arranged for a singer/musician to record the song. The faces, the cries, and the song stayed in my mind; it was overwhelming!

I made an appointment with our pastor, and I told him all of what I saw and heard. I gave him a tape of the song. He did not know what to make of my experience either. As time passed, I acknowledged that God had declared a vision to me, but I did not understand the significance of it. God is a patient God. I have learned that many years may pass before we understand a message from Him.

As mentioned previously, in 2005, my husband, Burke, died at the age of 53. Minutes after he died, he appeared in the home of Dr. Carl Willis. The night following his death, my husband appeared in the home of Dr. Arthur Cushman. Burke gave both doctors similar messages, saying that he had "gone to Heaven to be with God." He told them not to worry, that he was OK. The doctors shared their encounters with me.

The appearances to the two doctors and the messages my husband imparted were actually the inspiration that led me to write *Real Messages from Heaven*. This book offers hope and encouragement to those who have lost loved ones and to those who are uncertain about their salvation. It demonstrates there is life after death and there is a need to seek God while there is still time.

The experience of writing this book and being used by God as a tool reminded me of the Scripture from Jeremiah that I heard that night long ago. *"If you extract the precious from the worthless, you will become My spokesman."*

Death is the last enemy. When God allowed my husband to return with his message, God made it possible for a message of hope to be extracted from something as worthless as death! God gave me the strength and ability to share that message. Could I possibly be considered His spokesperson in that instance? I wanted to help those who were devastated by death. By way of the book, I believe God is using me to help others. Am I being obedient to God? He told me, "You give them something!" I believe God is giving them something through me.

It took 13 years for the vision to finally make sense! Then there is the matter of the song. I believe the song is Burke's message to me from Heaven, although God imparted the words to me before my husband died. I believe the song is a message to each of us from our loved ones who are now in Heaven. Is anything too difficult for God? You might want to read the lyrics and see if you agree.

## COATTAILS OF JESUS

### *Verse one*

*There are some things that I would say, if I were there with you,*
*Like dry your eyes and rest your mind, some things we can't undo.*
*I will always love you, we're apart for just a while,*
*Don't forget, there are no tears, in the presence of His smile!*

### *Verse two*

*The water in the river, of life never sleeps,*
*The banks are overflowing, with promises He'll keep.*
*So lift your head and look up, into a hope-filled sky,*
*Know that I'll be waiting, where we'll never say good-bye.*

### *Chorus*

*I'm holding onto the coattails of Jesus!*
*There's no chance of me letting go.*
*Inside the gates, there's no such thing as darkness,*
*No shadows in the Light that's white as snow.*
*Please go on believing in the Reason Heaven sings,*
*It wasn't God who took my life, but He gave me wings!*
*Last but not least, remind your heart to see,*
*You've not seen the last of me.*

Chapter 18

# Perfect Timing

When I awoke, the red digital numbers on the face of the clock glowed in the darkness; I distinctly recall the time read 4:44. I talked to the Lord until 5:30. At that particular time, I began praying for my daughter who was going through a flare-up of Sarcoidosis, a painful inflammatory disease that affects all major organs, including the eyes.

As I prayed, I thought of a conversation two years earlier with a woman who also suffered from Sarcoidosis. She had done extensive research on this disease and she learned much about available medical treatment. Most doctors have little experience treating Sarcoidosis, and the woman who came to mind possessed a wealth of potentially beneficial knowledge. I wanted to ask her some questions. I remembered her name was Kathy, but I could not remember her last name.

I had spoken to Kathy by phone, but I had never met her in person. I could not even remember who put me in contact with her in the first place; I had no way of finding her. I told the Lord of my desire to speak to Kathy and prayed, *"Lord, if You want me to talk to her, You will have to have her call me."*

Later that morning, I went to my daughter's home to take care of my young grandson. I answered the phone when it rang at 1:30 that afternoon. A voice said, "This is Kathy and I'm trying to reach Faye." The woman I had prayed to find only eight hours earlier had called my daughter's home to find me! Shocked that my prayer was answered so quickly, I asked her why she called and how she obtained my daughter's number. She said she was compelled to call me from the time she got out of bed that morning. Though not sure how to find me, she remembered the woman who put us in touch initially and gave her a call. The woman gave Kathy a phone number, not realizing it was actually my daughter's. Kathy dialed the number and, lo and behold, I answered the phone at my daughter's house.

Kathy felt certain she was supposed to share the name of an ophthalmic solution with me. Since it had decreased her eye symptoms significantly, she thought it might be beneficial to my daughter. I told her about my prayer and we were both amazed at how God works. He really does hear every prayer! Some answers come swiftly and others take time, but He hears every prayer.

At 5:30 that morning, while I was speaking to God, God was speaking to Kathy. He knew exactly where I would be at 1:30, so He provided Kathy with the number she needed to reach me at that precise time. God answered my prayer as I prayed!

God's ways are wonderful! Sometimes, I think He works in such ways to cause me to pause, look up, and ask, "What, Lord?" I can almost hear Him respond, "Did you get that? Do you think there is anything I cannot handle? Do you realize I know your every thought, your every word, and your every prayer, even before you pray?"

God works in mysterious ways!

Chapter 19

# Healed

Donna Layne knew she served a miracle-working God! She and our family prayed for God to remove a large cyst that was located in the very back of her throat, in the pharynx. We prayed and believed that God would heal her! The days and weeks passed and she experienced no change in her condition. The painful and annoying condition reminded her something was very wrong each time she spoke words or even swallowed food or water.

She scheduled an appointment with an ENT specialist. Dr. Reiber was a very personable man, and he seemed to be very knowledgeable in his field of expertise. He advised Donna to have an operation, allowing him to remove the cyst. She agreed to have the procedure.

I met our daughter, Donna, at the Surgery Center on the day of the operation. After registration, a nurse escorted Donna to the restricted surgery area beyond the lobby.

Perhaps an hour and a half passed before the surgeon appeared in the waiting room and approached me. He looked a bit confused, and he began to explain what just took place.

Dr. Reiber spoke in amazement, saying, "I went in to remove the cyst but it was gone! It was there, but it is not there now. She is waking up at this time, but she did not have surgery. Only an indentation remains, indicating something was once there. There is no need for surgery!"

I voiced my thanks to God and told Dr. Reiber how I believed in God's power to heal. I didn't understand why God chose to heal sometimes and not always, but I trusted His authority and His judgment. Dr. Reiber agreed with me, yet he seemed to be a little puzzled. Dr. Reiber and I both knew God had used him to document and authenticate a miraculous healing!

Donna was released from the medical facility and we went about our business with a sense of awe! It is amazing to witness God's extraordinary power! Donna was aware the cyst existed when she arrived at the facility—the cyst vanished between the time she walked out of the lobby and the time she walked back into the lobby!

Each of us knew we had experienced something astonishing and supernatural! How very like God to validate His exceptional work in regard to answered prayer by using an unsuspecting, scientifically minded physician as a witness. Many years have passed since that happened, but I still remember what an incredible experience that was!

*Oh Lord my God, I cried to You for help, and You healed me* (Psalm 30:2).

Chapter 20

# Can You See Me?

Courtney Bordelon lived with her doting parents, Gloria and James, in Sallis, Mississippi. It was a small, quaint town located approximately 15 miles from the historic Natchez Trace.

Courtney was no ordinary child; she was born an "old soul." While her friends watched cartoons, she avoided animated shows, preferring real people and real things. Courtney was shy and reluctant to carry on a conversation with strangers, but was open and affectionate with the people she loved. She was intelligent, witty, and usually the center of attention.

One day, Gloria was preparing to drive to the movie store in a nearby town. Four-year-old Courtney demanded she be able to dress herself for the trip. Rather than argue with the opinionated child, Gloria complied. Soon, Courtney came prancing from her room wearing mismatched colors, stripes, and polka dots, topping off the outlandish outfit with a huge bow on top of her head. With no further conversation, mother and daughter got in the car and began their short drive.

As they drove along Courtney asked, "Mama, how do I look?" Without looking at her daughter, Gloria assured her she looked fine. The highly offended child replied, "You haven't even looked at me!" Gloria reminded her outspoken little girl that she could not drive and look at her at the same time. Courtney did not miss a beat before she declared, "You don't know what it's like to be seventeen years old and trapped in a four-year-old body!" It was a hilarious moment, but that statement portrayed the real Courtney.

As she grew, Courtney remained a vivacious, precocious child. No one would have guessed she had been born with a genetic liver disease. Throughout her young life, she dealt with her disease with a courage and maturity that belied her years.

By the time she turned 15, Courtney had become a beautiful young woman with shoulder-length, sandy-colored hair, dark complexion, and big, brown eyes. However, it was obvious that living with the chronic illness had taken a toll on her. The disease had progressed alarmingly; the only thing that could save the young teenager's life was a liver transplant.

An acceptable donor liver became available, and Courtney received the life-saving operation. Hope flickered in the hearts of her loving parents. Their hope was short-lived when only a short time after the surgery, Courtney developed life-threatening complications. Courtney Bordelon died in September—on her mother's birthday.

Losing Courtney was devastating for her family. They loved her so much! Giving her up was the hardest thing they ever had to do. Gloria felt as if part of her body was missing. The pain deepened with each passing day.

About two weeks after the funeral, Gloria was awakened one night by someone shaking her leg and calling to her. She opened her eyes, sat up in bed, and was startled to find Courtney sitting on the foot of her bed, legs dangling over the side and swinging back and forth, as she had done many times before!

Gloria exclaimed, "Oh, I've been so worried about you!"

"Don't, Mama; I'm fine. I'm fine!" Courtney replied.

"Well, I can't believe you are here! Can you see me?" Gloria asked.

Courtney rolled her brown eyes at her mom and said, "Yes, I can see you; you can see me, can't you?"

Gloria smiled and said, "Yes, I can!"

Then Courtney replied sweetly and sincerely, "I didn't want you to worry."

Gloria told her daughter she loved her and Courtney responded with four precious words, "I love you, too." Courtney then faded from sight.

Gloria was stunned by the encounter, but comforted and filled with a calm, sure peace.

The certainty of being reunited with Courtney has given Gloria the strength to endure the heartache; and the memory of Courtney's after-death visit continues to fill her heart with hope and encouragement. Gloria's heart remains filled with the assurance that Courtney's spirit lives on in a better place; she has proof in the form of a miracle from God!

Chapter 21

# Angel Food

**B**urke Aldridge grimaced from the pain of lung and bone cancer; he slowly opened his eyes as he tried to make sense of regaining consciousness on day 21 of hospitalization. His eyes surveyed the small hospital room. He was uncertain of his surroundings. I gently explained to Burke, telling him he had been moved from the Intensive Care Unit back to the Critical Care Unit at Baptist Hospital in Nashville. The room in CCU provided less human interference from medical personnel and more privacy for Burke and our family.

Burke had not eaten in two weeks; on the last Sunday afternoon of his life, he announced, "I want something to eat!" Our son was present and exclaimed to his dad that he would go anywhere and find anything he desired. Burke said, "I only want a bite of something...I wish I had a bite of a SNICKERS® candy bar and a bite of cantaloupe." The Lord provided for Burke that day by undeniable godly and divine intervention.

One bite of a SNICKERS® candy bar and one bite of cantaloupe was Burke's last earthly meal. He wanted no more and no less. Earlier that same day, our daughter, Donna, came to the hospital to see her dad and she brought fresh fruit for me to eat, which I didn't eat. Fresh cantaloupe in a small, sealed container sat on a shelf by the sink; it took only seconds to grant half of Burke's request!

My childhood friend, Mildred Barrett, traveled 350 miles the day before to see Burke and brought a bag of snacks for me. I didn't know what the entire bag contained; however, I caught a glimpse of the word SNICKERS® when I moved the bag from ICU to CCU the day before. Sure enough, the bag rendered a package of bite-size SNICKERS® candy bars! Burke's wish came true in less than a minute!

I did not think it was strange that God supplied Burke's last meal before we or he knew he wanted it. It was merely evidence of God's personal touch! During those moments while David and I shared the food with Burke, I felt surrounded by the merciful and loving presence of an awesome God. I knew without question God was with us!

To this day, when I think of cantaloupe and SNICKERS® candy bars, I think of "angel food"! God provided angel food for Burke that cold February day, and I gratefully and publicly acknowledge His marvelous divine intervention!

> *Are not two sparrows sold for a cent? And yet not one of them will fall to the ground apart from your Father. But the very hairs of your head are all numbered. So do not fear; you are more valuable than many sparrows. Therefore everyone who confesses Me before men, I will also confess him before My Father who is in heaven. But whoever denies Me before men, I will also deny him before My Father who is in heaven* (Matthew 10:29-33).

Chapter 22

# Hope for Tomorrow

## PART ONE

Harold and Beverly Sutton were blessed with a near picture-perfect life. The happily married couple had three wonderful children: Wayne, a college sophomore; Ricky, a high school senior; and Ramona, their adored little sister. The Suttons were Christians, caring and giving people who were active in their church and community. Harold was a successful realtor and land developer in a booming real estate market. It seemed the Suttons had realized all their hopes and dreams for a contented, successful life.

Life was good for the Sutton clan; but life turns on a dime.

Life as the Sutton family knew it ended abruptly one horrible night. They received the devastating news that Wayne and Ricky had suffered a fatal automobile collision; both of their fine, young sons were gone. Death came suddenly; there was no time to say "goodbye."

Harold, Beverly, and Ramona had strong faith, yet they wondered how they could endure their tragic loss. The family came to understand the death of a child is one of the worst tragedies a human can bear.

In spite of their pain, the world kept turning and days turned into years. Life went on; but, for Harold, the grief remained unbearable. One morning he went to the cemetery and stood at the foot of the graves. His broken heart was filled with an unrelenting sense of loss that had grown more agonizing over the two years since the death of his sons. In tears, Harold spoke to the Lord. He acknowledged his sons were safe; he was certain they were in Heaven enjoying more than he could ever have given them on earth. But this father's heart could not find comfort. Harold cried out to God, "Lord, can You help me with this pain? It's more than I can stand!"

There was no audible reply to his cry; however, the crushing sorrow diminished instantly. Harold still experienced the pain of separation, but it was suddenly bearable. Harold was amazed!

He remembered a picture of a man walking along the seashore. Two sets of footsteps could be seen, imprinted in the sand along the path the man had walked. The story behind the picture suggests that Jesus always walks beside us although we cannot see Him. At critical times in our lives, only one set of footprints can be seen. Those are the times when Jesus picks us up and carries us in His arms because He knows we cannot go on in our own strength. Harold felt as though the picture had become a reality; Jesus, knowing Harold could not go on alone, had lifted him up and held him close.

## Part Two

Several months later, Harold attended a chamber of commerce meeting where an evening meal was served. While at the dinner, he developed severe abdominal, chest, and arm pain. Suspecting a heart attack in progress, friends rushed Harold to the fire hall in the small town of Mt. Juliet, Tennessee, and an ambulance was called.

It was almost seven o'clock in the evening, but much daylight remained and the area was well-lit. As they awaited the ambulance, Harold sat outside the fire hall in excruciating pain and struggled to breathe. His symptoms continued to worsen, and Harold realized he could be dying. He tried to fight the panic that arose by focusing on his surroundings. As he looked upward toward the roof of the fire hall, his deceased sons appeared!

Wayne and Ricky were sitting on the roof of the fire hall with their legs dangling over the edge, in the way one would sit on the tailgate of a pickup truck. They were dressed in white shirts, black tuxedos, black bowties, and black shoes, as if they were about to attend a formal gathering. They did not speak; they smiled continuously at their dad as their legs swung back and forth. Harold was overcome by a feeling of comfort and peace; he began to relax.

Harold thought, *If I die, I'll go and be with the boys, and if I live, I will stay here with Beverly and Ramona; in either case, I'll be OK!* He began to breathe easier and his pain diminished. Wayne and Ricky disappeared as suddenly as they appeared. In Harold's mind, the extraordinary occurrence seemed somehow normal and natural.

The ambulance arrived and transported Harold to a nearby hospital. He was treated and, after a few days, underwent successful heart bypass surgery.

The heart surgeon talked with Harold about the visit from his sons occurring at that crucial time. The surgeon explained that Harold's ability to relax during the heart attack had allowed much-needed oxygen and blood to circulate more freely. He concluded by saying, "I believe your sons saved your life."

Harold now looks back over all the fantastic events he experienced: God had comforted his heart and made the unbearable, bearable. The continued, vibrant life of his departed sons was seen by his own eyes. Harold believes these events were God's merciful way of saying, "Everything is OK. Continue to live your life to the fullest and to the very best of your ability. One day you will have My promise: You and your loved ones will be reunited and will be together for all time."

## Part Three

Shortly after Harold's graveside encounter, Beverly's uncle suffered a heart attack and died. Emergency measures restored him to life. He was angry when he came back from his near-death experience, exclaiming he had not wanted to return! "If you could only see what I saw, you would understand! The beauty of the sights and colors in Heaven were so extraordinary! The divine music was unimaginable and incomprehensible! I didn't want to leave it," he declared. He gave explicit instructions for the next time he died—no one was to bring him back. His family gave him full assurance that they would follow his instructions.

About one year later, Beverly was awakened one night by the sound of Harold crying in his sleep. Assuming he was dreaming of their deceased sons, she gently woke him. But Harold's dream was not filled with the grief of death; it was an encounter with life after death!

Harold dreamed of being in a strange building resembling a duplex. He stood in a doorway of the structure, watching his deceased son, Wayne, as he approached. Wayne appeared to come over a lush, grassy hill, walking toward Harold, who was delighted to see his son's smiling face. When Wayne reached the building, he turned and entered an alternate door. When he reappeared, he carried something in his arms, but Harold could not see what it was.

Wayne retraced his steps and walked back across the grassy slope. He repeatedly looked back over his shoulder at his dad. Just before he disappeared from sight, Wayne stopped, looked back with a smile on his face, and waved to his dad! Harold asked him to come back for just a minute; he wanted to hear his son's voice and look into his eyes. Harold's tears were caused by his son's silent refusal to stop and talk with him.

Ten minutes after the dream, Harold and Beverly received a phone call. They learned that Beverly's uncle had just died and, this time, no one attempted to resuscitate him. Apparently, the death and the dream happened at the same time. Harold felt relieved; he was convinced Wayne was sent to escort his uncle beyond death's door. Could it be Wayne now serves God by guiding people to Heaven?

# Chapter 23

# Poppa Tall

When innocent, small children see angelic beings, how can we possibly doubt? My granddaughter, Reese Isabella, was a year and a half old when her beloved Poppa passed away after a brief illness. I recall watching the two of them together a month before his death. My husband, Burke, and Reese appeared to be the only two people in the room—and in the whole world for that matter!

Burke sat in a chair and played the guitar for Reese. He sang Little Red Caboose for her repeatedly at her request. Reese stood directly in front of him with a tiny hand on each knee. When the music stopped, Reese squealed and asked for more, "Sing, Poppa, sing! Play tah, Poppa!" A "tah" was a guitar in Reese's world.

The music and laughter between them was a beautiful thing. Reese danced, laughed, and captivated the heart of the man she knew and loved as Poppa. When the music was over, he picked Reese up and held her close; then Burke lifted her high above his head while she laughed until she was out of breath! Precious memories.

One month after that musical afternoon, my husband died at Baptist Hospital in Nashville on a Monday evening around midnight. I called our son and daughter and asked them to come to the hospital at once. I did not tell them Burke was dead until they arrived in the room where I waited for them with Burke's body.

My son's wife, Rhonda, later told me how she went in to check on Reese when our son, David, left that night. Reese always slept on her belly with her knees drawn underneath her body. That night was different. Rhonda quietly peered into the crib and discovered Reese was asleep on her back with her little head tilted back, chin and lips extended forward. Rhonda said she knew at that moment that Poppa was dead, that he had stopped off to kiss his lovely little granddaughter good-bye.

A few weeks later, David, Rhonda, and Reese were relaxing on their screened-in back deck when Reese began to laugh and point excitedly. Her tiny finger pointed to the top of a row of trees along the back property line. Reese laughed with joyful laughter and innocently exclaimed repeatedly, "Poppa tall! Poppa tall!" She saw what the others could not see.

On more than one occasion, Reese's parents observed her sitting in the middle of the bed, laughing and talking to an invisible Poppa. Each time they watched in amazement as she jabbered in baby talk and carried on what appeared to be a one-sided conversation to the observer. Children under the age of two don't know how to lie or deceive. She saw what she saw as an innocent child and responded honestly and openly. She is older now and has no recollection of the incidents; however, we will always remember, with much love and appreciation to God for His remarkable gifts!

*And Jesus said to him, "...All things are possible to him who believes"* (Mark 9:23).

# Chapter 24

# A Message of Hope

Laura* grew up in the Church of Christ. She knew about Jesus and had often heard the message of salvation. However Laura spent most of her life running from God, refusing to accept His free gift of new, abundant life through His Son.

Determined to live her life according to her own rules, Laura ran head-long into a lifestyle of self-destruction. She became a drug user and, ultimately, a drug addict. When her funds were exhausted, Laura became a prostitute to fund her habit. Tomorrow was never on Laura's radar; she spent her days in efforts to feed her growing addiction.

Circumstances intervened in Laura's wasted life when she learned she was dying of cancer. Impending death cast a shocking clarity to her shattered life and meaningless existence. Laura was filled with shame and regret. She began to realize her need of God. Laura's bruised and hardened heart became more tender and open; she was ready to accept God's salvation—she was ready to follow Jesus.

Laura's doctor admitted her to Baptist Hospital for treatment to prolong her life. Chaplain Lewis Lamberth visited her often during her stay. He spent time getting to know her and telling her about Jesus. He explained to her how Jesus died on the cross for each of us so our sins would be forgiven; he told her the blood of Jesus covers all sin. Understanding began to dawn on Laura; God's truth became a beacon of hope.

Finally, Laura prayed a simple, but heartfelt prayer. She asked God for forgiveness and accepted Jesus as her Savior and Lord.

After Laura committed her life to Jesus, she wanted to do all her newfound Lord required. Having never been baptized, Laura felt a strong need to do so. She wanted to make a statement about her decision to follow the Lord and to confirm her new life in God. Chaplain Lamberth was more than thrilled to comply with her wishes.

Soon after her baptism, Laura left the hospital with a new hope in spite of her dire prognosis. She lived for only a few more months before returning to Baptist Hospital to die.

After Laura's death, her sister-in-law contacted Chaplain Lamberth and told him an interesting story. She and her husband were lying in bed asleep on the night of Laura's death. It was about ten o'clock in the evening when she awoke to see Laura standing near the foot of the bed. She looked 20 years younger than her actual age and she was dressed in white clothing. Laura said, "I'm OK, don't worry!" She said nothing further before she faded out of sight. Laura's sister-in-law immediately phoned the hospital. The nurse informed her that Laura died only minutes before.

Laura's sister-in-law knew Chaplain Lamberth was instrumental in Laura's conversion. She believed Laura wanted him to know that she had indeed made it to the other side and was in Heaven, doing just fine!

Chaplain Lewis Lamberth, Jr. is still doing God's work. Today he is the Director of Pastoral Care at Baptist Hospital in Nashville, Tennessee.

*A fictitious name was used to protect the identity of the deceased.*

# Chapter 25

# LOVE Clouds

Our youngest grandson, Daniel, was only six years old when his grandfather died the end of February in 2005. We celebrated Daniel's seventh birthday two weeks later. I will be very honest; it wasn't much of a celebration. My daughter, Donna, tried her best to carry on with a cake and party for little Daniel, but the smiles were all make-believe for Daniel's sake.

I watched Daniel that day because in addition to being brokenhearted, he acted in a peculiar manner. He walked through the house peering into each room and into closets. He spoke words just above a whisper, and I could not tell what he was saying. I began to walk closely behind him, and I listened carefully to his words. He appeared to be playing hide and seek, a game he and Poppa played many times.

When I realized what he was saying each time he looked into a new possible hiding spot, my heart broke for that precious little boy. Daniel's eyes searched everywhere as he softly spoke, saying, "Poppa, you can come out now! It's my birthday, Poppa; please come out now!" I thought my heart would break that day, and I'm sure Daniel felt the same way. Hugs, kisses, and the words "I love you" were all I could give him. I am sorry to say I fell short of consoling him in a significant way. Sometimes we as humans have nothing to give in times of grief except our presence. In those terrible times, it is important to remember that God is with us!

Springtime appeared slowly that year. The green rye grass, yellow buttercups, and purple hyacinths pushed their heads out of the cold ground and the sunshine offered glimpses of hope that our world was still turning. I remember one warm day in late March when Daniel was visiting me at the farm; he played on his little green tractor under the carport as I worked in the kitchen.

Suddenly, I heard Daniel calling to me! Mothers and grandmothers can tell by the tone of voice if a shout is one about pain, fear, or excitement. Daniel's shout was all about excitement! He shouted for me to come quickly. I heard him say something about the sky. I hurried outside to find him standing firmly planted and pointing toward the western sky of blue. Daniel told me to "Look!" and I did.

To my astonishment, I saw the word *LOVE* in the beautiful blue sky. Each letter hung in the sky in the form of a billowy, white cumulous cloud. I became as excited as Daniel! Could this really be? Yes, it was very real! Both of us witnessed it! The letters began to lose shape almost as soon as I realized we were not dreaming. *"And the witness in the sky is faithful"* (Ps. 89:37).

A gentle breeze caught the letters and swept them into one large, fluffy cloud! A heavenly artist was at work! In Daniel's seven-year-old mind, his Poppa was saying, "I love YOU, Daniel!" Daniel needed that more than anything that day. Who else but God could offer that sweet child love and hope from the heavens above? That was an amazing display of compassion and extraordinary love unlike anything I had ever seen.

According to the Bible, God manifests His holy presence in the clouds. He certainly did that day!

> *… When they praised the Lord saying, "He indeed is good for His lovingkindness is everlasting," then the house, the house of the Lord, was filled with a cloud, so that the priests could not stand to minister because of the cloud, for the glory of the Lord filled the house of God* (2 Chronicles 5:13-14).

# Chapter 26

# Crown of Life

The Pitchford family of Patton, Missouri, became complete when Mary was born. Sadie, her loving mother, adored the tiny infant. Her desire to protect her daughter blossomed full-grown the moment she held the baby in her arms. With great care, she gently placed Mary on a soft feather pillow for her first contented nap.

Mary grew into a vibrant toddler, bringing joy and laughter into the Pitchford home. All too soon, Mary outgrew her little pillow bed; but she fell asleep each night with her tiny head nestled into its comforting folds.

In the winter of 1911, two-year-old Mary fell extremely ill. Although Sadie diligently tended her frail daughter, her constant love and care were not enough to save little Mary's life. On the tenth day of December, Mary's vibrant spirit left her body. Her tiny head rested for the final time on the little feather-pillow bed.

The joyous season of Christmas was at hand, but it was grief, not joy, that filled the Pitchford home. The memory of Mary's sweet little voice seemed to echo in the empty house like a sad love song, ending with good-bye.

In the days following Mary's death, Sadie became emotionally attached to that little feather pillow. She often found herself holding it closely in an attempt to fill empty arms that felt useless and awkward in the absence of her child.

One day as Sadie caressed the pillow, she noticed a lump inside that had never been there before. She had fashioned the pillow herself; she knew it contained only an abundance of soft feathers. Quickly, Sadie cut the pillow open and was amazed to discover a strange, artistically formed object. Hidden deep within the pillow was a flawless, extremely beautiful, white feather crown! The little crown was about four inches in diameter and two inches tall; it would have fit Mary's head perfectly.

The Pitchford family had no explanation for the extraordinary work of art. They accepted it with an attitude of faith, believing it to be a gift from God. To them it symbolized the crown of life little Mary had received from God's loving hands. The little crown became a reminder that Mary was in God's perfect care for all time, and the cloud of grief became easier to bear. As the years passed, amazement and gratitude replaced the sadness in their hearts.

The little feather crown is now in the possession of Sadie's great-grandson, Bruce Watkins, of Hendersonville, Tennessee. A century has come and gone, yet the gift of hope remains in impeccable condition and is revered by the Watkins family.

## Chapter 27

# Love You, Love You, Love You

It was the day after Christmas when I became severely ill. At the time, I still lived on the farm, and I had recently had my kitchen updated with granite countertops and new appliances. The kitchen looked fabulous, so I decided to redo the paint on the walls myself. I worked for days standing on a tall ladder with my neck turned at a precarious angle. I painstakingly painted the trim, and it took a very long time. I'm a perfectionist, so I painted and repainted until I was exhausted! Breathing the paint fumes didn't help either. The kitchen looked so pretty that I decided to paint the great room and the foyer too. I did not use good judgment when I decided to do the painting. I was forced to abandon my efforts and call a professional painter to finish the job!

When I awoke the day after Christmas, I could hardly stand up! My head and neck ached! I could hardly breathe. I had no strength at all. I thought a little rest would make me better, so I went back to bed.

My condition did not improve with time and rest. After January 1, I went to my physician and he ordered tests and prescribed medication. My symptoms grew worse and worse. The problems all started with painting my kitchen! I did not want to alarm my family and, honestly, I thought it might be time to go home to Heaven. My husband had been dead for two years, and I was not happy. As a child of God, I did not fear dying. Heaven became more inviting by the minute.

On the 27th day of January, I went to bed wondering where I would wake up. Something extraordinary happened that night!

What I remember is this: I saw my deceased husband, Burke, in an expanse in front of me. He looked at me, then moved beyond my sight. In a few moments, he was standing clearly in front of me only 10 or 12 feet away. I left my bed, and *I did not walk* to get to him—I stepped into his world momentarily. I was suddenly there, and I don't know how I got there!

Burke wore a white shirt with short sleeves and cut-off blue jeans. That is what he wore when he cut the grass, and that is what he wore that night. I hugged him, and he hugged me. I felt his warm cheek against my cheek! His body was warm to touch and his body was solid matter. He felt no different in my arms than he did when he was alive on earth!

My face was against his face when he spoke to me and said, "Love you, love you, love you!" Burke always signed greeting cards he gave me that way. I was startled and delighted to hear his voice, and I pulled my face back and looked into his eyes. His dark brown eyes sparkled! His smile was radiant as he looked at me intently. He was the picture of perfect health, peace, and happiness. I felt like all was right in the world once more.

I said to him, "Can I go with you?" Burke replied, "You have to stay for now, for the children." I blinked my eyes, and I was back in bed inside that achy body! That is exactly what happened, but I cannot explain how it happened. Perhaps I died for a couple of minutes then returned to my body. I believe that is what happened, but I cannot prove it. The experience was real. I was wide awake when the experience began and when it ended.

I clearly received God's message! He sent it through Burke with an encouraging and affectionate hug. I experienced God's love, kindness, and compassion firmly—yet in all His gentleness! I knew I had to get better and stay on earth to accomplish my purpose. I knew God had plans for me and plans for my life.

The year was difficult, but I steadily regained my strength and fully recovered. God has been so generous and kind to me in my lifetime, and not because I am deserving of His gifts, but because He is a loving Father. The Lord is everything to me, and I am very thankful to Him for His presence in my life and in the lives of my family. I can never thank Him or praise Him enough!

## Chapter 28

# A Servant's Heart

A sense of freedom and purpose stirred in Jaimee Underwood as she traveled toward Knoxville, just east of Nashville, Tennessee, on Interstate 40. She was a single mother of two small children and a successful criminal defense attorney living in Franklin, Tennessee. Jaimee was a strong-willed woman who recently survived a painful divorce and premature death of her father whom she dearly loved. She went through some tough emotional times but with much determination, she seemed to be getting her life back on track.

Instinctively, Jaimee focused on the positive, looking forward to a great weekend. Her thoughts drifted toward the anticipated reunion with her six-year-old daughter, Alexa, and her two-year-old son, Lawson. They had spent a week with their dad and Jaimee was anxious to see them.

The date was July 19, 2004 and the time was approximately 6:30 in the evening. Jaimee was driving in the far left lane of four eastbound lanes of traffic when she ran over a small object that punctured her tire; she pulled the huge SUV to the left shoulder of the road into an extremely narrow space between the heavy traffic and a large, concrete barrier. The flat tire was on the passenger's side, nearest the oncoming traffic. Jaimee realized the danger of her situation. She reported her predicament to her motor club and contacted the Tennessee Highway Patrol for assistance.

Police officer Christy Dedman responded to the call. She pulled her patrol car close behind Jaimee's vehicle and activated the emergency lights of the cruiser. Everything was by the book—the scene was a textbook example of safe procedure employed in an effort to divert traffic around the disabled SUV long enough for Jaimee to change the tire.

Jaimee looked into the smiling face of Officer Christy Dedman, and they both tried to remain calm in the face of their precarious dilemma. Seconds later, Jaimee found herself lying flat on her back, dazed, confused, and in excruciating pain. An eastbound tractor-trailer rig, traveling at approximately 70 miles per hour, crashed into the back of the patrol car, which in turn crashed into Jaimee and Officer Dedman.

A 250-pound piece of the demolished police car pinned Jaimee against the pavement. Her breathing was limited and her pain was indescribable.

An off-duty truck driver came to Jaimee's aid. He knelt down beside her and noticed she appeared to be unconscious; however, her eyes were open. Small pieces of crushed glass filled her motionless eyes. He could not believe she was alive. The stranger gently picked the glass out of Jaimee's eyes with his fingertips.

An off-duty paramedic emerged from one of the cars in the traffic that backed up for several miles due to the accident. Jaimee feared she was dying, but the paramedic assured her she would be all right; the expression on his face said otherwise. Jaimee began praying she would live long enough to say good-bye to her children and family. The paramedic stayed with Jaimee until help arrived, holding her head so she could not see the body of Christy Dedman lying motionless beside her. The impact of the crash killed Officer Christy Dedman instantly.

An ambulance arrived and transported Jaimee to the trauma ward at Vanderbilt Medical Center in Nashville. She was critically injured and losing blood at an alarming rate; however, she remained awake and aware during the entire ordeal, resisting the ever-present urge to allow darkness and oblivion to render her unconscious.

Jaimee sustained a traumatic brain injury, lacerations to her spleen, liver, and kidney, and an "open-book" pelvic fracture that shattered her pelvic bone into three pieces. The internal bleeding was profuse, requiring numerous blood transfusions. Jaimee's pelvic fracture necessitated surgery. Large screws and metal rods affixed to her pelvic bone literally held her together. After suffering a collapsed lung on two separate occasions, Jaimee's condition stabilized.

One of Jaimee's nurses was exceptionally kind; she went beyond the call of duty to be helpful. One morning shortly after the accident, the nurse shared an extraordinary account with Jaimee. "When I was with you in your room last night, I felt Christy Dedman's presence very strongly. I finished cleaning you up, and I went to the sink to wash my hands. When I looked in the mirror, I saw Officer Christy Dedman standing behind me. She was standing there, smiling at you! She was dressed in her uniform and hat." The nurse told Jaimee, "When I turned from the mirror, Christy vanished."

Jaimee's nurse reported seeing Officer Dedman in Jaimee's room on several occasions over the next few days. Christy appeared calm, and she smiled whenever she appeared. Each time, Christy vanished when the nurse turned to look directly at her.

Morphine, a strong painkiller, was used to control Jaimee's relentless pain, leaving her thinking somewhat impaired. Jaimee wondered if her impaired thinking was the reason Christy appeared to the nurse instead of her.

To make matters worse, Jaimee suffered terribly from survivor's guilt; she was emotionally devastated. She could not understand why God spared her life and not Christy's. Jaimee's grief was tremendous and she felt responsible for Christy's death because Christy died helping her.

Christy's after-death appearances offered comfort to Jaimee and Christy's family. The appearances helped Jaimee understand that Christy did not blame her, and that Christy forgave her! Jaimee was able to deal with her grief over Christy by knowing she was still very much alive and in a far better place.

Jaimee's recovery did not happen overnight, but she did recover. Jaimee said, "The experience was a powerful thing that changed my life. Before the accident, I acknowledged God; however, I did not appreciate or serve God. I have come to a point in my life where I have truly accepted Jesus as my personal Savior. I accepted Jesus and received baptism at the age of fourteen, but I drifted away from my spiritual life. The wreck was a turning point. Because of all that happened to me, I have reconnected with Jesus in a profound way! I 'get it' now!"

Jaimee attends regular worship services and believes she is a better mom, a better lawyer, and a stronger Christian because of the adversities she has faced in her life.

*Officer Christy Dedman died at the age of 35, leaving behind her parents, a brother, aunts, uncles, cousins and many friends. She was the second female police officer to be killed in the line of duty in Nashville. The Nashville Police Department posthumously awarded Officer Dedman the highest Medal of Honor bestowed by the Nashville Police Department—the Medal of Valor. Today a simple cross on Interstate 40, just east of Nashville, marks the place where Christy's life in this world ended tragically.*

Chapter 29

# Dylan's Mission

Dylan is an exceptional five-year-old boy. He is loveable, witty, intelligent, and funny! Surprisingly, Dylan is able to share detailed accounts of his visit to Heaven when he died at birth. Dylan matter-of-factly tells about when he was in "outer space" with God and he was "nothing but colors." Dylan claims he was "one blue and a bunch of purple." According to Dylan, God told him He was going to "send him to earth on his mission". God then touched him and Dylan turned green and then an orange-red color. The next thing he knew, he was in his mother's belly.

(Dylan's mom, Dana, was curious about the significance of the colors he described so vividly. She looked up the meanings of the colors: Blue is spirit, purple is royalty; green is life and the orange-red that he described to his mom is indicative of flesh.)

Dana awoke one morning during her third trimester and was heading for the shower when her water broke. The realization that her baby was about to be born a month early was undeniable. Dana arrived at the hospital and her first few hours were uneventful. The nurses carried out standard procedures while Dana focused her mind on staying calm during the anticipated birthing experience.

Nothing could have prepared Dana for what was about to happen! Warning bells sounded to alert the medical staff the baby was losing vital signs and the amniotic fluid was drying up. Fluids were added and nature took its course. When push time came, Dana and her doctor learned the baby was stuck in the birth canal and he could not be born the usual way.

The doctor chose to attempt a forceps delivery. The forceps slipped and the first attempt failed. The doctor tried again. This time the forceps took hold with a vengeance. A loud crack echoed through the delivery room and by the look on the doctor's face, Dana knew things had gone horribly wrong.

Nurses immediately rushed Dana into surgery. The operating room lights were off as they wheeled Dana in. Dana squeezed her eyes shut when the bright lights suddenly lit up the room. Nurses scurried, bringing out equipment in preparation for the surgical procedure about to take place, even though the anesthesiologist had not yet arrived. Many strong hands held Dana down and the cutting began. In pain, she bit the arm of the emergency room doctor who worked to save the tiny baby. Dana apologized for biting the doctor as she bit him, and his response to her was, "You do what you have to do, and I'll do what I have to do."

Dana awoke the next morning in a hospital room with an empty bassinet beside her. Her heart raced and unwelcome thoughts flooded her mind. She was informed that her newborn son, Dylan, had been flown to another hospital with multiple skull fractures and swelling of the brain from the forceps. Dylan had been clinically dead for over four minutes. The swelling in his head had been so extensive that even in the x-rays, he looked like he was wearing a traffic cone on his head.

The swelling went down; the skull fractures healed, but the brain was damaged from the loss of oxygen. For the first year, trips to the neurologist were a testimony to God and His power to heal. Early MRIs showed that Dylan should have no ability to function. He functioned. There were delays in motor skills and milestones, but he functioned. As Dylan grew and the delays were more noticeable, Dana suspected cerebral palsy. She had done the research and he had symptoms. By the time he was four, the brain showed what Dana suspected and the diagnosis was confirmed. Dylan's official diagnosis was mild periventricular leukoma, also known as cerebral palsy, and common in cases of brain injury and loss of oxygen. The brain cells die off and are replaced with air. The only way to accurately diagnose it was with an MRI, where gaps would be evident in the brain matter.

Dylan could walk and run, but there was a noticeable limp and rigidity in the left side. At five years old, Dylan was able to function normally with his right arm and leg, but had weakness in his left side. He had trouble climbing stairs and had balance issues. Dylan's family had been warned there might be behavioral issues and trouble reasoning; however, his behavior and reasoning proved to be normal for a five-year-old. When told by a physical therapist that he needed to practice hopping on his left foot, Dylan's response was a simple, thought-out reply, "I don't think that is a skill that I am going to need."

Soon after Dylan's fifth birthday, he awoke in the middle of the night, holding his head and hollering, "It's all better, my brain is back!" Dana laughed at her young son and told him he was silly. Shortly after that night, Dana took back her words.

Dylan was scheduled for an MRI to identify why he was having headaches. After the procedure, Dylan's neurologist met with his family and told them, "Although a child's brain can adapt to cell damage by finding alternative routes that bypass the damaged areas, the white matter normally does not grow back. Dylan now has the brain of a normal five-year-old child." The doctor showed the family that where there were once gaps of air, there were now living brain cells. That was miraculous!

Five-year-old Dylan still shows symptoms of CP, but his family is confident that with therapy and God's infinite power, he will gain full function of his motor skills in the near future.

Recently, Dana was driving when out of the blue Dylan said, "You know Jesus died, huh?" Dana told him she knew that and Dylan continued, "He came back alive though." Dana was surprised because although they had started introducing him to the stories of Jesus, they had not told him about the resurrection because they were afraid it might be too difficult of a concept for him to grasp. Dana asked Dylan how he knew that and he said, "He (God) told me…He also said you are going to run out of gas if you don't stop at a gas station soon." Dana laughed because where Dylan was sitting did not allow him to see her gas gauge. As she started laughing, her gas light came on! She immediately stopped for gas.

# Chapter 30

# Divine Journey

As he did every day, Alvin Glenwood Watkins (Glen) climbed aboard the long yellow school bus and began his assigned route through the streets of Farmington, Missouri. A veteran bus driver, Glen was cautious, and he drove the huge vehicle with care, always aware he carried precious cargo. Glen never failed to consider the well-being of the children as he picked them up and took them home each day.

This day began like any other day. As he expertly maneuvered the bus filled with 66 children, Glen was unaware that he had embarked upon a very unexpected, divine journey.

All was routine, and the bus traveled uneventfully along when, without warning, Glen experienced a terrible, crushing pain in his chest. He pulled the bus to the side of the road and engaged the emergency brake before he collapsed and fell across the steering wheel. Glen suffered a massive heart attack. A student ran to the nearest building and called for help.

Glen's body remained inside the bus, but his spirit took flight to another land. As realization dawned, Glen found himself standing before an awesome archway. The breathtaking structure marked the entrance to a land of beauty beyond words. As he looked through the archway, Glen saw an unending field of brilliantly colored flowers stretching out in all directions. The colors were vivid, rich, and indescribable! Each flower was unique, perfect, and superior to anything he had ever seen on earth. Glen experienced an extraordinary perceptive ability; he knew, without being told, he could not go beyond the gates. Somehow, he was acutely aware it was not his time; he was compelled to return to his life on earth.

Glen survived the heart attack; though his body was seriously weakened, he slowly recovered. He later told his son, Bruce, about his near-death experience. Glen was absolutely certain he had died and arrived at the gates to Heaven!

The beauty Glen saw, the peace he felt, and the joy that filled his soul became memories so precious, so personal, and so cherished that he could barely speak of his experience. With tears streaming down his face, Glen said, "Human words seem to degrade the holiness of the experience." Glen found it impossible to adequately convey what he experienced; the story of his divine journey was rarely told. Glen stored the memories within his heart and cherished them for the rest of his life.

Over 30 years later, Glen suffered another heart attack and passed from this world. Glen's son, Bruce Watkins, recalls the strange mixture of emotion he experienced during his father's funeral. The separation from his dad was heartrending, but Bruce had such an overwhelming peace and assurance about his father's destination that he found tears seemed somehow unwarranted. Just before Glen's casket was closed, Bruce looked at his dad one last time and said, "Dad, I hate to see you go." Still, there were no tears. Bruce could almost hear his dad reply, "Don't cry for me, son. I'm fine!"

Bruce is convinced, beyond a shadow of doubt, his father has now crossed through that breathtaking archway. Glen has experienced the inestimable joy of entering Heaven through those marvelous gates! One can only imagine the joy Glen experiences each day as he kneels at the feet of Jesus, the One who died on the cross. Enveloped in the unspeakable peace and love of that holy place, Glen has now begun a new life—a divine journey in the Kingdom of God.

# Chapter 31

# White Feathers

I hugged my 16-year-old grandson just before he left the church and handed him a BP gas card. Jacob owned his very first car and had been driving for less than a week. He grinned and thanked me. Jacob kissed me on the cheek before he drove away that morning on his way to see his girlfriend.

After attending early service, I went into my Sunday school room for class. After class, a young woman ran to me and said, "Jacob has been in an accident! Have you heard?" My heart skipped a beat, and I ran to my car to find my phone!

I learned that Jacob was traveling on an unfamiliar road in search of a BP gas station when the accident occurred. Jacob in his car and a woman in her car both arrived at an intersection at precisely the same moment. They were traveling at speeds of approximately 45 miles per hour when they crashed. Both vehicles were instantly totaled! Each car contained one occupant, the driver. Only by God's grace, each driver walked away from the accident without a scratch.

Jacob's mom, Donna, arrived at the scene of the accident shortly after it happened. My daughter hugged her son and looked him over, making certain he was all right. She looked at Jacob's demolished Volvo in horror. The safety airbag deployed on impact.

My grandson said, "Mom, I never knew airbags were filled with feathers!"

Donna replied, "There are no feathers in airbags! They are filled with air. Why do you think they are filled with feathers?"

"When I crashed, I saw white feathers all around me! White feathers were flying everywhere and were all over the seat!" Jacob exclaimed.

Donna said the peace of God, which surpasses all comprehension, filled her at that moment.

> *And the peace of God, which surpasses all comprehension, will guard your hearts and your minds in Christ Jesus* (Philippians 4:7).

Donna explained to Jacob, "Since you started driving, I having been praying for God to keep you safe, and each day I plead the blood of Jesus over you—and I claim the 91st Psalm over you!"

> *He who dwells in the secret place of the Most High shall abide under the shadow of the Almighty. I will say of the Lord, "He is my refuge and my fortress; my God, in Him I will trust!"...He shall cover you with His feathers, and under His wings you shall take refuge....For He shall give His angels charge over you, to keep* [guard] *you in all your ways* (Psalm 91:1-2,4,11 NKJV).

Jacob jokingly but truthfully remarked, "So angels really do have feathers! White feathers!" Jacob was amazed when he realized God's hand of protection had surely saved him and the other driver! *The presence of the white feathers seemed to stress the fact that God wanted Jacob to remember who saved him!*

Upon further inspection of the car, Jacob's mom noticed a small crushed section in the lower passenger side of the windshield. It appeared that a passenger's head had landed there, except for the fact there was no passenger! Jacob and our family believe an angel was riding with him at the time of the crash and for that, we are forever grateful to God!

# Chapter 32

# A Very Good Thing

Some people just stand out in a crowd; 15-year-old Scott Rule was undoubtedly unforgettable. With blonde hair, blue eyes, and freckles, he had an endearing face that was often lit by an easy smile. Scott was extremely popular among his friends. Everyone loved this lively teenager who lived life to its fullest.

Scott lived in Laramie, Wyoming, with his parents, Dan and JoAnn Rule. His older sister, Jennifer, also lived and worked in Laramie while attending the University of Wyoming as a full-time student.

On July 7, 2001, Scott and his parents set off on a short trip to the Wyoming State Fair in nearby Douglas, Wyoming. Rather than ride in his parents' car, Scott decided to accompany his friends on the drive to Douglas. Scott was riding in the back seat of the small car when it entered an intersection and was broadsided by a pickup truck. Scott was severely injured by the massive impact.

Jennifer was at work when her mother called with the horrifying report. Her brother was in critical condition in the Douglas hospital; he was fighting for his life. Jennifer immediately left for Douglas.

When Jennifer arrived at the hospital, she learned Scott had been taken by helicopter to the state's only level-one trauma unit, located in Casper, Wyoming. Her father's broken heart was obvious as he gave Jennifer the devastating news: Scott never arrived; he died during the flight. Jennifer's voice echoed against the hard, cold hospital walls as she screamed, "He's too young! He's too young!" Angry tears filled her eyes as pain and loss pierced her heart.

Scott's body was returned to the Douglas hospital and the family stood around his lifeless form. Jennifer's heart was further wounded as she watched her mother gently shake Scott's feet and plead with desperation, "Scottie, wake up! Please, wake up!" Jennifer was overcome by sorrow; the shock and pain had left her nearly unable to breathe.

After her parents left the room, Jennifer was alone with her little brother's body. He was lying on a gurney; he looked so different. Jennifer spoke to Scott in a way only a big sister can: "Scott, I need you to be with me. I need you to help me take care of our parents. I need you to help me get through this!" Jennifer stood looking at Scott and slowly calmed her raging emotions. She bent over her brother's beloved face and gently kissed his cheek. Suddenly she felt a strength that was not there just moments before. She dried her eyes and left the room. No one saw her cry after that tearful farewell.

Scott's funeral service reflected a life well lived; over 600 people attended. The Roman Catholic sanctuary could not hold all the people who came to grieve with the family and to celebrate the life of the special person who was Scott Rule. His life had touched so many people! His death reminded them of what had been; it brought into focus the truth of eternity and Scott's new life in Heaven.

A couple of weeks after Scott's death, Jennifer lay sleeping alone in her room. She was lying on her back when something brought her abruptly awake. She opened her eyes to see Scott standing at the foot of her bed! He did not speak; he just stood there quietly, looking directly at Jennifer. Scott was wearing a red baseball jacket (he had always loved baseball) and dark blue jeans. Both his hands were in his pockets as he stood patiently before her, making sure she knew he was there. Jennifer could not believe what she was seeing. She pulled the bedsheet over her head and closed her eyes. When she opened her eyes again and peered from beneath the sheet, he was no longer present; however, Scott's appearance had made a lasting impression.

Eight years have passed since Scott's accident. Jennifer Dible is now a nurse practitioner in Nashville, Tennessee. The passage of time has made reality somewhat less painful, although Jennifer still loves and misses Scott. Looking back, Jennifer says the loss of her brother and the experience of actually seeing him after his death made her faith grow. She remembers: "When I was growing up, going to church was just something you always did. After Scott's death, I became closer to God, and my spirituality increased more than I could ever have imagined."

The Rule family accepts Scott's after-death appearance as a special gift from God. The visit left Jennifer with peace of mind and hope; in her words, it is "a very good thing!"

# Chapter 33

# He Leadeth Me

I backed my SUV out of the garage hurriedly and drove toward Mt. Juliet, Tennessee. I was supposed to visit a Women's Club meeting at Lake Providence Del Webb Community that day. I was running late, and five minutes into the trip, I realized I did not have the directions to where I was going! I knew the name of the street for the first left turn, but that was all I remembered.

I drove and I prayed! I did not get upset. I talked to the Lord as I made my way through traffic, not really knowing what I was going to do! When I came to the recognizable turn off the main road, I laughed out loud and spoke audibly to the Lord, "Lord, I know Kenny Martin is the guest speaker at the meeting today. It would really be great if You would send Kenny to show me the way!"

I heard no reply but at that precise moment my eyes were literally drawn to the tag on a black SUV ahead of me. My eyes felt like metal drawn to a magnet! I could not read the tag, so without taking my eyes off the tag; I accelerated and closed the distance between the two vehicles! When I got close enough to read the letters on the tag I was overjoyed! The letters on the tag were the abbreviation for Mt. Juliet Chamber of Commerce. All I had to do was play follow the leader!

Kenny Martin was employed as the Economic and Community Development Director for the City of Mt. Juliet at the time. I knew Kenny had to be one of the two men in that black SUV in front of me. As soon as I asked, my heavenly Father answered "OK." He did exactly what I asked Him to do!

I followed the SUV to the security gates at Lake Providence. When the driver stopped for the security guard to check the guest list, I lowered my window and said to the guard, "I'm going where they're going!" He waved me through; I know he wondered why I was laughing, especially since I appeared to be alone. I am never alone! God was with me, and I believe He was laughing too.

Kenny and his companion parked in the same area where I parked. I followed them to the club room.

When should we pray? If it matters to you or me, it matters to God. I believe our prayers are music to God's ears!

> *Pray without ceasing; in everything give thanks; for this is God's will for you in Christ Jesus* (1 Thessalonians 5:17-18).

# Chapter 34

# Twice Blessed

Mary Cole was oblivious to the magnificent display outside her bedroom window. When autumn comes to Knoxville, Tennessee, it has the surreal beauty of a picture postcard. During the annual transformation, vibrant rainbows of red, yellow, and orange will stretch across the hillsides. However, the pain in Mary's heart blinded her to all but the heartbreak of loss.

Mary Cole sat with a Bible in her lap. Only two months before, liver failure had claimed the life of her 32-year-old son, David. The separation was still new to her; time had not yet begun to ease the grief that filled her heart. She found special solace and strength in the Word of God. She had soaked up the Scriptures like a sponge that day as she diligently sought the Lord and His peace.

Suddenly, Mary became aware she was not alone in her room. She lifted her head to see that a very large being sat just in front of her. Mary realized she beheld an angel! It was solid white and sat with its chin in its hands, looking at Mary. The entity vanished after a moment; but Mary was certain of what she had seen. The angel had not spoken, but Mary was sure the angel was sent to comfort her in her time of need. She experienced a profound peace that surrounded her like a warm blanket, and her heart was comforted.

Several years passed and Mary's hunger for the Word of God continued unabated. Intense Bible study became a way of life for her, and most days found her poring over God's wonderful Word.

One day as Mary stood ironing, she felt a presence. She realized a Man stood next to her. His appearance was pure white, from head to toe. No garments accounted for the color; He appeared to be formed of solid, white matter. She heard no words but knew intuitively the Man was Jesus! He remained for only a few seconds, but long enough for Mary to comprehend the significance of the visitation. Again, as when the angel appeared, she was engulfed in an overwhelming peace.

Over the years, Mary has remained humbled by, and grateful for, the heavenly visitations. She is quick to acknowledge that her gifts were awesome and sent by God. Mary strongly believes her spirit was open to receive those visits because she had been immersed in the Word of God prior to each. Mary says, "By staying close to, and in tune with, God, I believe we stay open to direct communication with Him."

# Chapter 35

# Peace That Surpasses All Comprehension

I sat at my desk one day in late autumn; I worked but found it difficult to concentrate. I was concerned about a complex matter involving a unique individual and myself. By way of the Holy Spirit, I knew the Lord wanted to bless this individual, using him in a similar manner to the manner in which He used Paul in Biblical days. Paul was converted and changed from Saul to Paul. After that conversion, Paul lived his life only for the glory of God, encouraging others to follow Jesus. I believed God was using me as His vessel, to pray for my friend, 'Paul'. I had been standing in the gap for nearly five years, praying and believing! My faith was intact but I was weary and anxious to see my prayer answered.

I completed the story I was working on and I felt strongly that I should close that story with a verse of Scripture. The Scripture was Philippians 4:7 and I recalled the words to the Scripture but not the address. *I typed these words: And the peace of God, which surpasses all comprehension, will guard your hearts and your minds in Christ Jesus.*

I wanted to get the words down correctly so I double-checked. I looked in my Bible concordance and located the Scripture address. I closed the concordance and reached for my Bible. I opened the Bible with one motion and the Scripture was immediately before my eyes! I did not look for it or thumb through pages. One flick of my wrist, and I read the words from the Bible that I just typed on my keyboard then read from my computer screen!

I thought to myself, *God surely caused that to happen!* Before I finished that thought, the phone rang. I answered and heard a pre-recorded message from a Prayer Ministry. The voice said, *"Pray for the peace that surpasses all comprehension..."* I recalled Paul, by way of the Holy Spirit, in the Bible, wrote Philippians. *Through Divine intervention, the Holy Spirit was comforting and encouraging me by echoing Paul's words to me in reference to the 'Paul" I was praying for!*

When the call ended, I thought, *God is so amazing! My left hand is still on the Bible and my finger is pointing to those same words!* My right hand rested on the phone receiver God used to speak the same words into my ear. My eyes stared at those same words on the computer screen. I received the same Scripture multiple ways in less than two minutes!

I recalled the matter over which I was perplexed only moments before; my worries no longer existed. My emotions were actually expressions of doubt. *Faith will not work when there is doubt.* At once, my faith grew stronger and I realized that *God cared about my friend even more than I did!* In my mind and spirit, I released my friend into God's hands. I believed, by faith, that God would settle the matter His way and in His time. I said to the Lord, *I will not give up-I will pray and trust until it happens!*

I thought to myself; *how many of life's failures are people who did not realize how close they were to success when they gave up?*

# Chapter 36

# Peace

Kathy Dedmon was the Wilson County Building Inspector for many years. She watched as the sleepy, rural Tennessee county changed over the years from a simple farming community into one of the fastest growing counties in the nation. In early 2009, Kathy retired after a long and successful career. She now takes great pleasure in caring for her grandchild, and Kathy never fails to enjoy and appreciate life.

This is Kathy's story.

In April 1987, Kathy and her husband, Kenneth Ricketts, lived in Watertown, Tennessee. The couple was busy building their lives and making a home for their little family. Without warning, the couple's life together came to an abrupt end. Kenneth suffered a massive heart attack and died in the bedroom of their home. He was only 40 years old.

Over the next two months, Kathy experienced denial and anger. Each day seemed an eternity. Grief and confusion so overwhelmed her that Kathy feared for her own sanity. But there was no escape from the reality and finality of Kenneth's death. Kathy tried to remain strong for her family and, finally, found a degree of acceptance for a circumstance over which she had no control.

One night in early June, Kathy fell asleep next to her son in his bed. The six-year-old often had trouble sleeping in the months following his dad's death. To comfort him, Kathy would lie down beside him until he drifted off to sleep. The night was quiet, and Kathy and her son had finally fallen into a deep sleep. Suddenly the sound of someone entering the room awakened Kathy. When she turned to look, a familiar yet disturbing sight met her gaze; Kenneth, her deceased husband, was sitting beside the bed!

Kenneth was wearing a light blue shirt and dark blue pants. He reached out his hand and touched Kathy. She could not feel the touch of his hand, but watched as he gently patted her. Kenneth told her, "Kathy, quit worrying. I'm OK." Then Kenneth was gone. The brevity of his stunning appearance left Kathy with no time or inclination to respond.

Afterward, Kathy sat quietly in the darkened room. She contemplated life and death and the separation between the living and the dead. She could not explain or fully understand the visit from her undeniably dead husband; but she experienced no fear or apprehension. Kathy searched her heart to discover her innermost feelings following the encounter. The only word to describe the calm, gentle acceptance that flooded her being was "peace."

# Chapter 37

# We Walk by Faith

In 1981, God called Bill Walters into full-time ministry working for The Gideons International. Bill, his wife, Lois, and four children moved from North Carolina to Nashville, Tennessee, where the Gideons headquarters is located. The organization is an extended missionary arm of the church and its purpose is to win the lost for Christ. One way this mission is pursued is through the distribution of the Word of God. Countless souls have come to know Jesus Christ as Lord and Savior through this extraordinary ministry! The Gideons have distributed more than 1.6 billion Bibles and New Testaments around the world since their founding in 1899! In 1990, Bill got the opportunity to represent the Gideons in a visit to Albania.

In 1967, Albania became the first ever atheistic claimed country in the world. Religion had been officially banned! The very act of talking about church was prohibited. The churches themselves were torn down, burned, or made into museums. All people had to denounce their faith or be executed or imprisoned. People who tried to leave the country were executed, and their families were persecuted. Faith lived in the hearts of a small number of believers—but they dared not speak of it. They prayed in the dark of night and made the sign of the cross in seclusion.

Tirana is the capital city of Albania and home to 607,467 of the country's 3.2 million people. Albania is located in southeastern Europe. It is bordered by Montenegro to the northwest, Kosovo to the northeast, the

Republic of Macedonia to the east, and Greece to the south and south-east. It is less than 45 miles from Italy.

Bill Walters was one of the first Americans allowed in the country after the fall of communism. He went there as a "tourist." Bill's goal was to explore the opportunities of organizing the Gideons there. He arrived in Tirana, having flown in from Rome. He was aware there were five fellowships (churches) in the country. His mission was to visit all five to possibly meet businesspeople and professionals who were born-again believers in Christ Jesus. Bill needed to enlist six such men if he was to successfully start the Gideon ministry there.

Bill believed with all his heart that God would accompany him on his mission; God made His presence known several times while Bill was in Albania. When Bill arrived in Tirana, he discovered there was a $15 fee to enter the country, and he carried only one hundred dollar bills. He stood still, contemplating what he should do. If he paid with a hundred dollar bill, he would get no change; they had no American currency. Bill needed the money in his wallet.

An English-speaking American woman appeared as if by appointment! She graciously paid customs the fee, which allowed Bill to enter the country. The woman was waiting for a man coming in from Germany. She was in Albania to help restructure the Albanian government that had collapsed during the communist reign. With the fall of communism, the country was in shambles, and Albania was in need of a totally restructured government.

God sent the same woman to help Bill a second time the same day. She saw his predicament and offered to take him into the capital city along with the man from Germany. God's timing was perfect! Bill felt God's wonderful presence and understood he was not alone in that lonely place.

Bill checked in at his hotel by five o'clock. A short time later, he left the hotel seeking the first fellowship. He had no earthly idea where it might be. He walked by faith, trusting God to make a way for him to find it. A stranger approached Bill and offered assistance. Bill explained his need and the young man showed him the way to the first fellowship. It was a divine appointment! Later, the man walked Bill safely back to his hotel. *"Are they* [angels] *not all ministering spirits, sent out to render service for the sake of those who will inherit salvation?"* (Heb. 1:14).

The next day, the same man returned, and by the end of the day, he and Bill had visited the other four fellowships! It was not permissible to call them churches at the time. The stranger accepted Bill's thanks, but refused Bill's offer to pay him for his time even though everyone there lived in dire poverty. By the end of the second day, Bill had the names of five possible candidates, three of whom were military officers. There was only one problem; no one knew how to find any of the military officers.

Bill did have actual directions to one contact, and he walked until he located the flat that matched his directions. When he knocked on the door, Bill was greeted by a man who broke into a broad smile then ran back into his house leaving the door open! He quickly returned with a small white Gideon's Medical Testament! He pointed to the Gideon emblem on the Testament then to the Gideon pin on Bill's coat!

Bill said, "He hugged me and he kissed me because he knew I represented that book! The book represented Jesus Christ, He invited me in and we talked!" The man spoke in broken English, and he told Bill he was not aware of another adult businessman, born-again believer in the entire country! Six men were needed and only one was found. Bill left his newfound friend and promised on behalf of the Gideons, "We'll be back!"

In 1993, a Gideon from the British Isles went back to Albania with Bill's detailed summary, located the one man Bill had met and was able to locate five additional men, with all six completing membership applications! The first Gideons Ministry in Albania was formed in August 1993! Since 1993, the Gideons have distributed over 400,000 copies of God's Word in Albania. God is faithful!

Bill Walters planted the first seed of faith in Albania in 1990 with God's help. As Christians, we never work alone; it is always a joint venture with our heavenly Father!

> *According to the grace of God which was given to me, like a wise master builder I laid a foundation, and another is building upon it. But each man must be careful how he builds on it. For no man can lay a foundation other than the one which is laid, which is Jesus Christ* (1 Corinthians 3:10-11).

# Chapter 38

# I'm Free

Agnes Johnson lived alone in her Orlando, Florida, home. A widow with few friends and no family in the area, Agnes spent many lonely hours. To fill her time, Agnes bought a small, blond-colored organ and set about teaching herself to play. Before long, beautiful music brightened Agnes' small world.

In 1981, Agnes received a wonderful surprise; her niece, Judy, was moving to Orlando.

Jim and Judy Johnson were eager to get the move underway. They wanted to relocate to Orlando for some time and the right job opportunity now paved the way.

Jim, Judy, and their two sons were excited to begin a new chapter in their lives, but ending the old one was difficult. They were saddened to leave their many friends in Wausau, Wisconsin; especially the members of their little mission church. The members were almost like family, all depending on one another for survival. Preparing for the move was a bittersweet time for the young family.

Once they got settled in their new home, Judy set about getting to know her widowed aunt. Having family live nearby was a novel and welcome change. Their extended family was small, so the Johnsons had always relied heavily on God, faith, and friends to fill their need for love and support. Since they knew no one else in the area, Aunt Agnes represented both friend and family to the transplanted Johnson clan.

Before long, Judy realized Agnes did not attend church services and didn't seem to be affiliated with any of the area's many churches. The fact concerned her, but she kept her thoughts to herself.

Though she did not attend herself, Aunt Agnes urged Jim and Judy to visit St. John's Church. The pastor, Dr. Bob Hawk, had presided at her husband's funeral and left quite an impression on her. The Johnsons had already visited several churches in the area, each time with no inclination to return; so they quickly agreed to visit St. John's.

Dr. Hawk was on vacation when the Johnsons first visited his church. A member of the congregation acted as a guest speaker. The subject of his sermon was loneliness. The message brought tears to the Johnsons' eyes because they desperately missed their Wisconsin home, church family, and friends. They were extremely lonely in their new home and needed to become connected to a new body of believers. Judy remembers, "We were so alone, and we just didn't feel needed anymore."

The following Sunday, the Johnson family attended services at St. John's and were pleased to see Dr. Hawk had returned to his pulpit. After hearing him preach, they agreed unanimously that St. John's would be their new church home.

A short time after Judy and Jim moved to Florida, Aunt Agnes developed brain cancer. Judy became her primary caregiver, assisting Agnes as she suffered through the trying ordeal. The cancer progressed rapidly. Agnes endured a craniotomy to remove the tumor, and six weeks of agonizing radiation therapy followed. Agnes' condition deteriorated severely. Realizing Agnes could no longer live at home, Judy facilitated her move to a long-term care facility. Judy lovingly cared for Agnes and fed her the last meal she had on earth before she lapsed into a coma and died in the autumn of 1982.

Following her aunt's death, Judy was plagued by questions. She wondered what happened to Agnes when she died. Was Agnes in Heaven? Had she done the right thing as a caregiver? Should she have spoken to her aunt about the Lord? At that time, Judy's concept of a Christian was a person who attended church regularly. Since she had never known Aunt Agnes to attend a church service, Judy was not sure where her aunt stood with God. She had always been too hesitant to inquire but had prayed diligently for her critically ill aunt. Judy longed to know Agnes' fate, but it seemed the answer to that all-important question would never be known.

The only people who came to Agnes' funeral were Jim, Judy, their two sons, and Judy's parents. Before the funeral, Dr. Hawk led them in prayer.

What happened next was simply amazing. The following account is in Judy's own words.

"While we were praying, I saw a vivid picture of Agnes clearly and unmistakably in my spirit and mind! I saw Agnes in an expanse above me, as if she were in a thought bubble above a cartoon. There she was, a few feet above me, seated at her organ, playing music! The organ looked very much like the one she had at her home…Her fingers were flying across the keyboard! Her feet were moving on the pedals and she was looking over her shoulder at me! She had the most beautiful smile on her face and she shouted down at me, 'I am free! I'm not locked in this body anymore!' There was color. Her hair had a red tint. In life, she had a round face. In her after-death appearance, her face appeared round and full once again. She was wearing all neutral colors: pale white and light browns. I remember she was wearing a beautiful blouse! I don't remember what her shoes looked like. She looked so pretty—very young, radiant, and healthy! It was almost like looking in a window of Heaven!"

All Judy's doubts about Aunt Agnes' destination were dispelled by the incredible display of God's mercy and grace.

After the funeral, church members came to the Johnsons' home to visit and bring food. Their presence was needed and appreciated by the Johnson family. They formed new relationships; they had finally found a new church home.

Judy's Aunt Agnes was perhaps an isolated, un-churched Christian, but a Christian, nonetheless. Her godly wisdom guided Jim and Judy to St. John's Church. Judy says she will always be thankful for the after-death appearance of her Aunt Agnes; it was a very special and very welcome gift from God!

Chapter 39

# Against All Odds

J effrey Chaffin grew up in Lebanon, Tennessee, a small town just east
of Nashville. The rural community held no future for Jeffrey, and he
possessed a wandering spirit. He was a young adult when he took
to the highways in search of a place that felt like home. Jeffrey hitch-
hiked all across America, working for brief stints, then moving on to new
locations.

Jeffrey made a few rare appearances back home over a 20-year span.
His visits were never long enough. In 2003, Jeffrey found himself living
and working on the West Coast. Jeffrey suffered critical injuries when he
fell from the tallest point of an escalator to the concrete floor below in
May 2003. He suffered multiple broken bones and a severe closed head
injury. The blow to his head rendered him unconscious immediately.

The emergency room physician admitted Jeffrey to the Intensive
Care Unit for treatment. He remained in a coma and showed no signs of
improvement. His physician ordered an EEG and the results indicated
that Jeffrey was brain dead; there was no hope for his survival.

Estelle Chaffin, Jeffrey's grandmother, lived in Mt. Juliet, Tennessee.
When she got the news, she was devastated! Her age and physical limi-
tations did not permit her to travel to the other side of the country to
see her beloved grandson. She wept as she recalled his childhood and
troubled years. Mrs. Chaffin stood in her yard beneath the giant limbs of

a shady hickory tree as she shared the sad news with me. We had been friends and neighbors for many years.

I encouraged her not to give up hope but to believe against all odds that Jeffrey would live in spite of the doctor's prognosis. Mrs. Chaffin cried as she told me that Jeffrey's parents were already making funeral arrangements, preparing to have his remains transported back to Tennessee.

I tried to comfort Mrs. Chaffin, and we prayed for Jeffrey as we stood there in the shade. We asked God to heal Jeffrey and to raise him up and give him life again! After a long visit, we each returned to our homes.

Several days passed, and I called to inquire about Jeffrey's condition. I was surprised and overjoyed by Mrs. Chaffin's wonderful news! She told me she had just received a phone call about Jeffrey. She said, "This morning Jeffrey sat up, and he is talking! He ate breakfast! The doctors don't know what to think!"

It is not every day that the dead is raised, but that day was Jeffrey's day to be raised up and restored to life! God's divine intervention restored his body and breathed life into Jeffrey. God answered our prayer! Distance is of no significance to God. Two thousand miles stood between the two people who prayed and the man who received the answer to that prayer; however, God was in both places! He is all-powerful!

*Behold, the Lord's hand is not so short that it cannot save; nor is His ear so dull that it cannot hear* (Isaiah 59:1).

# Chapter 40

# Reunion

Susie Covington Austin lived in Springfield, Tennessee, with her husband, Tom (Big Daddy) Austin, until he died in November 1980, at the age of 66. They had owned and operated Austin Bell Funeral Home for many years.

In 2004, at the age of 85, Susie suffered a heart attack and never fully recovered. She wanted to remain in her home but was too weak to care for herself. Susie's daughter, Marcia Echols, and her granddaughter, Susan Echols, agreed to take turns staying with her. Both of them lived in Nashville at the time.

Marcia knew her mother was a Christian by the way she had lived her life. They had discussed salvation, and Susie was confident she would one day enjoy God's presence in Heaven. However, Marcia struggled to let her mother go. She prayed, "Oh God, I need confirmation about my mother. The most important thing in the world to me is that all my family will be up there in Heaven. That's all that really matters."

Following that prayer, Marcia's mother, Susie, had an extraordinary dream. When she awoke, she realized she had been to Heaven! In a voice filled with obvious excitement, she told her daughter, "Guess who was waiting for me at the gate? Big Daddy and Jesus! Big Daddy said, 'I thought you would never get here! I've been waiting for you!' It was wonderful to see him. Then we all went inside, and I saw Mama and Papa and many loved ones!"

Susan asked her grandmother if the streets of Heaven were really made of gold. Susie replied, "Susan, there was gold everywhere! I saw what looked like pearls. It was so beautiful I cannot even describe it. I'm convinced I was really there—in Heaven!" Marcia was certain her mother's dream was the confirmation she had requested. She was finally able to release her mother into God's loving care.

On the weekend before Susie's death, the Lord gave Marcia an inner certainty that her mother's earthly life was about to come to a close. And it appeared her mother was also aware of her imminent death. Susie's strength seemed to rally throughout the weekend. She called many of her friends and relatives for brief conversations, telling each of them good-bye and assuring them of her love. Susan and her grandmother stayed awake most of Sunday night, reminiscing.

On Monday afternoon, Susan left her grandmother's home at 5:00 and Marcia arrived at 5:30. Susie died in that 30-minute span while she was alone. When Marcia arrived, she found her mom in bed, her upper body elevated and arms extended. Marcia said, "From her position, I would say she saw someone and reached out to go with that person. She was still reaching out when I found her." Marcia gently repositioned her mother's still body into a reclining position.

Marcia recalls, "Mother died the week of Thanksgiving and was buried that weekend. It was a sad holiday without her, but all her family was so thankful to God for blessing us with a godly mother. Many family members and friends came to the funeral to celebrate her life. Mother experienced her own reunion in Heaven with all her loved ones from past generations."

Susie Austin realized dying is a natural part of life; and she faced it alone, sure of the reward to come. For her, death held no fear or pain. Death is only painful to the ones who are left behind.

# Chapter 41

# Immanuel

In September 1978, Ken and Joy Clayton found themselves serving as missionaries in Spain when an unprecedented time of testing came upon them. Joy gave birth to their son, Kenny, on September 12. A week later, Joy became very ill with bronchitis. A village doctor treated her at home, but Joy became weaker and sicker with each passing day. It was clear that something was dreadfully wrong!

Ken bundled up his wife in the car along with four-year-old Jill and baby Kenny. They set out to find the doctor who had delivered Kenny. When they reached the clinic, the doctor took one look at Joy and confirmed their suspicions that Joy's condition was life-threatening. The doctor suspected typhoid fever or hepatitis. Ken took Joy to the hospital in Vigo where the doctors admitted her for treatment of one of the worst cases of hepatitis they had ever seen. Ken had no choice but to leave her at the hospital and drive home with their two children.

Three days after Joy went into the hospital, Kenny became extremely ill with a severe stomach virus. Ken carried his infant son to the hospital where he stayed for 11 days. Two days after Kenny went to the hospital, four-year-old Jill became very ill with hepatitis. The doctor allowed Ken to care for Jill at home as long as she remained at complete bed rest.

Ken desperately needed some assistance; he could not leave Jill for a moment, and she was too ill to leave her bed. A neighbor recommended a teenager whose name was Milagros. She lived several miles away but daily walked to the village where she bought food supplies. Ken arranged for Milagros to come to their home each day to bring food from the market and to prepare a meal for them. She was able to care for Jill when Ken needed to go to the hospital to see Joy and Kenny. Ken was able to visit Joy on one occasion before he returned to the hospital to bring little Kenny home.

Ken was frightened as he drove the winding two-lane road from Vigo to their house on the coast above Portugal. It was a 30-kilometer trip. Little Kenny lay swaddled in blankets on the floorboard of the small Spanish car. Ken was anxious about caring for the tiny, frail baby. Four-year-old Jill was at the house in the village with Milagros; she was too sick to travel. Ken had never seen anyone as sick as Joy recover.

When they arrived home, Kenny cried excessively. He developed an intolerable case of diaper rash from which there was no relief. Ken sang to the baby and rocked him for hours in an effort to console his son. The baby slept for 30 minutes and cried for three hours routinely. Ken became physically and emotionally exhausted as he continued to care for his family. He remained in a constant state of prayer. Ken and Joy's families and several churches in the United States were praying for them.

Joy went into the hospital in mid-September and was still there when November came. Kenny was not well and he cried much of the time. Jill still required care and attention. One afternoon, Ken sat rocking the baby so that he could rest. While he was praying, Ken accepted the fact that they were in a terrible time of testing.

The biblical experience of Elijah and the prophets on Mt. Carmel came to Ken's mind. Ken prayed aloud, "Lord, we are standing every day on Mt. Carmel with Elijah and the prophets." He reaffirmed that belief several times. His mind then skipped to the part of the story where Elijah was in the cave. Elijah felt very much alone. Ken felt like Elijah.

Ken prayed in earnest! His tears fell on the face of the beloved child he cradled in his arms. He was not sure how much longer they could endure the intense suffering. Ken was not sure any of his family was going to survive. The awesome voice of God illumined Ken's darkest moment when God spoke aloud to him, saying, *"My son, why are you crying? I have promised to BE with you!"* If another person had been present in the room at that time, he or she would certainly have heard the same spoken words that Ken heard. The words were not whispered; they were spoken audibly! God was there in the room watching, listening, and speaking to His child Ken Clayton!

Ken said, "A great peace flooded my soul. I realized the Lord had not promised to heal Joy, Jill, or Kenny; however, He was with us! That was all that mattered. I don't know why He spoke to me, but I suppose it was because He knew I needed Him so much at that moment. He came to my rescue! I was absolutely overwhelmed with gratitude." There was hope!

Milagros stayed with the children the next day while Ken went to the hospital to tell Joy what happened! Before he could tell her, Joy anxiously exclaimed to Ken, "Yesterday afternoon I felt the Lord's presence in this room like I have never felt it before!" Ken and Joy cried together as Ken shared with her about God's very real visit and audibly spoken words to him! Joy then said, "It is going to be all right, isn't it?" Ken replied with strong conviction, "Yes!" God had visited Ken in the village and Joy in the hospital on the very same afternoon! God made His presence known to each of them simultaneously.

In December, the Claytons returned to Tennessee on a medical furlough while Joy recuperated. Kenny was almost a year old before Joy regained enough strength to care for him. More than a year passed before Joy regained the strength to push a vacuum cleaner across the room. Ken lovingly cared for his family until they were well again; he perfected his cleaning and cooking skills during those trying times. By God's grace, the Clayton family survived!

Dr. Ken Clayton, a Baptist minister in the Nashville, Tennessee, area, remains convinced today that the experience changed his life. It changed his perception of the Bible. He believes the central message of the Bible is God's desire to be in a *close, personal relationship* with each one of us. God's desire was climaxed by the coming of Jesus, our Immanuel, *"God with us"!* At Pentecost, the Holy Spirit came to dwell in us. Dr. Clayton declares, "From Genesis to Revelation, the Lord is declaring His desire to *BE* with us! So many personalities of the Bible were encouraged by God's promise to *BE* with them from Abraham and Moses to Joshua and all the way to the disciples and the Great Commission!"

What a promise! *"I am with you, always!"* That is what Ken needed to hear that long ago, but not forgotten, day in Spain. That is what we all need to hear, even now!

> *...Behold, the tabernacle of God is among men, and He will dwell among them, and they shall be His people, and God Himself will be among them, and He will wipe away every tear from their eyes...* (Revelation 21:3-4).

Chapter 42

# The Little People

The temperature was 88 degrees, and the sky was clear and blue. As Ruby Seagraves drove through the streets of Orlando, Florida, it seemed she was taking a trip through paradise. Her mood was cheerful, and she was thoroughly enjoying the day. She had just left her optometrist's office with a good report; all was right in her world.

Both of Ruby's parents had died years before. Her father, Ernest Ash, died from cancer in 1997, and her mom, Opal, died of complications from Parkinson's disease in 1999. The couple had been openly affectionate throughout their long life together; their enduring love for one another had been obvious.

Ruby cared for her mother after her father's death. Feeling helpless, she could only watch as the Parkinson's disease ravaged her mother's body. Near the end, the disease progressed to the point where Opal's breathing was severely impaired. Ruby couldn't bear seeing her mother suffer. Watching her struggle just to breathe was heartrending. She reminded her mom that Heaven was waiting, and so was her husband. Opal passed away filled with the hope of being reunited with her beloved Ernest.

Ruby's thoughts were far from her deceased parents on that beautiful, spring day; nothing could have prepared her for what was about to take place.

Without warning, Ruby's mom and dad suddenly appeared in the car with her! They looked just as Ruby remembered them, except for one major detail: They were small enough to fit onto the dashboard of the car! They sat silently between the steering wheel and the windshield, directly in front of Ruby's awestruck eyes! Opal was wearing a floral print dress with a black background. Ernest wore a white shirt and dark pants. Opal sat on a chair resembling a stool, and Ernest stood behind her with his hands on her shoulders. They were both smiling!

Surprisingly, Ruby was not frightened; the extraordinary occurrence seemed, somehow, perfectly normal. She eagerly spoke to her mom, "Hi Mom! I've been missing you. I love you!" Next she spoke to her dad, "Daddy! I love you, too!" Her parents just smiled up at her, without speaking a single word.

As suddenly as the two appeared, they disappeared! Ruby continued her drive home with a sense of joy and awe.

The incident took place several years ago, but the details remain vivid in Ruby's mind. Prior to the experience, she would not have believed such a thing possible. However, Ruby's faith increased, and she has been encouraged by her parents' visit. When asked to sum up the incident in one sentence, Ruby slowly shook her head, smiled, and said "What a gift from God!"

# Chapter 43

# Final Instructions

Sandi Trabert was heartbroken when she learned her best friend, Mary Jane, was dying from lymphoma. When Mary Jane learned she was dying, she called Sandi and invited her to go to church with her and her husband, Bob. Sandi was very hesitant at first. She reluctantly accepted the invitation to meet her friends at church. Before long, the threesome was meeting every Saturday afternoon at 4:00 for church service. They had dinner together after each service, and Sandi enjoyed the time they shared. Mary Jane appeared to have a real need for Sandi to be in a relationship with God. Sandi did not make the commitment to return to church on her own; she only went at the request of Mary Jane. Sandi lived apart from God for 30 years, and she wondered if God would grant her His forgiveness.

The night Mary Jane passed away proved to be a memorable night for Sandi Trabert. Mary Jane calling her name awakened Sandi from a sound sleep! Sandi sat up in bed and was surprised to see the deceased Mary Jane in her bedroom. Mary Jane appeared to Sandi in the form of white mist. She hovered above Sandi's bed and spoke audible words to her. Sandi felt like she was in the midst of a holy angelic presence. The feeling was one of perfect peace, and Sandi wished the feeling would last forever.

Mary Jane said, "Sandi, I want you to take communion at my funeral service."

Sandi replied, "What do I do? It's been such a long time!"

Mary Jane told her to call a particular church and ask for a particular priest. Sandi was not familiar with the priest; however, she agreed to do as Mary Jane requested. Mary Jane then told her friend that she should announce an act of contrition, which is a recitation spoken after a confession is made in the Catholic Church. Thirty years had passed since Sandi spoke the words of contrition. Strangely and obediently, Sandi sat up in bed and said the words to the act of contrition word for word, not stumbling or at a loss for words. The deceased Mary Jane vanished at that time.

Sandi called Bob early the next morning and shared with him what happened during the night. He was amazed! Bob confirmed he knew the priest and the church Mary Jane spoke of in her after-death appearance.

Sandi proceeded to call the church and she related the encounter to the priest. Sandi told him she needed to go to confession because her deceased friend wanted her to receive communion. He replied, "Child, I believe what you say happened. I will be happy to meet with you for confession." Sandi arrived 30 minutes before the funeral and met with the priest. After she talked with him and prayed for forgiveness for her previous sins, she received communion and felt an incredible sense of peace and forgiveness from God.

After Mary Jane's death, Bob and Sandi shared the loss of a wife and a best friend. Their conversations led them to believe Mary Jane was preparing Sandi to become a Christian companion for Bob in her absence. Mary Jane had confided in her daughter that she did not want Bob to be alone; she wanted him to marry Sandi. Sandi's salvation was so important to Mary Jane that she made an after-death appearance to persuade Sandi to get her life right with Jesus Christ. The after-death appearance was the very thing that caused Sandi to take action, to repent and ask for God's forgiveness. In the months after the funeral, Bob and Sandi developed a very close friendship. Bob and Sandi married and lived happily as husband and wife for eight years before Bob died of an aneurysm.

Sandi lives her life today as a strong Christian, knowing Heaven is a real place. She does not fear death because she has experienced God's miraculous power and love in her life. One glimpse into the hereafter by way of her deceased friend still serves as a reminder that life does not end with death for the believer. Death is only the beginning!

> *Let not your heart be troubled; you believe in God, believe also in Me* [Jesus]. *In My Father's house are many mansions; if it were not so, I would have told you. I go to prepare a place for you. And if I go and prepare a place for you, I will come again and receive you to Myself; that where I am, there you may be also* (John 14:1-3 NKJV).

# Chapter 44

# A Mother's Love

In early 2009, Chuck began to complain of chest pains and an irregular heartbeat. Never one to allow much to stand in his way, Chuck attributed his health problems to the pressure he was under at work and kept going, full-speed ahead. Chuck owned a successful travel agency; it was his pride and joy. Owning the business was rewarding but proved to be incredibly stressful at times.

Adding to the stress was a giant portion of grief and confusion that defined much of Chuck's life. He had experienced many painful emotions since his mother, Debbie, died at the young age of 49.

Debbie made some regrettable choices in her life that negatively affected her relationship with Chuck. Most of Chuck's life was spent separated from his mother, and his grandparents had assumed primary responsibility for raising him and his sister. For as long as he could remember, Chuck had been at odds within himself where his mother was concerned. He loved her, but hated the effect her choices had on her family. Chuck longed for a loving, close relationship with his mother, but over the years, that relationship remained a dream, never a reality. It wasn't until the last two years of his mother's life that they were able to develop a semblance of the relationship Chuck craved.

One spring night in 2009, Chuck was awakened at three o'clock in the morning by severe chest pain and an alarmingly abnormal heartbeat. When he collapsed in the hall, his wife, Jamie, called 911. The ambulance arrived and the paramedics immediately put Chuck on a gurney and wheeled him to the ambulance. The doors were left standing open as they started an IV and placed a nitroglycerin tablet under Chuck's tongue. As he lay on the gurney, Chuck wondered if death was near. His eyes searched about fearfully, as if looking for an answer.

Suddenly through the open ambulance doors, Chuck saw an unimaginably bright, white light. In the midst of the light, Chuck could see his mom's face!

Chuck remembers, "She was standing there at the back of the ambulance, watching me."

Chuck saw only the upper portion of Debbie's body. In life, she had suffered from a condition that caused the muscles on one side of her face to droop. Chuck recalls that her younger-looking, beautiful face glowed; all evidence of the disfiguring condition was gone. Debbie looked absolutely radiant and the picture of health.

Debbie stood looking at her son, tears filling her eyes, and spoke one word, repeating it compassionately, "No, no, no." Chuck somehow knew his mother was saying "no" to his death; she was telling him to live. Her countenance was that of a loving mother, tenderly caring for a beloved child. Chuck interpreted her tears as tears of joy, tears from a grateful soul that had found the right road home. Chuck finally felt loved by his mother, and his heart was filled with hope and peace! He understood it was not time for him to leave this life. As the realization took hold in Chuck's mind, Debbie slowly faded from his sight.

Chuck was taken to a nearby hospital for treatment and experienced a full recovery.

Chuck is certain his mother is in Heaven. He believes she came at that crucial time in his life to demonstrate her love for him and encourage him to live, and quite possibly, to save his life!

# Chapter 45

# Angel in Cozumel

In the summer of 1993, Bruce Karcher left Louisiana and flew to Cozumel, Mexico, for a long-awaited scuba diving trip. Cozumel is truly one of the most breathtaking destinations in the world for scuba divers. Bruce was an avid diver at the age of 40. Cozumel is home to more than 20 miles of coral reef and a myriad of sea life. White sand, crystal clear ocean coves, and warm water created the perfect environment for snorkeling and scuba diving.

On the last day of the trip, Bruce decided to do some sightseeing away from the tourist attractions. He rented a motor scooter and set out to explore the rugged landscape and scenic surroundings. He enjoyed seeing the tropical terrain of Cozumel.

Where the asphalt road ended and the gravel road began was where Bruce decided to turn back and return to his hotel. He applied his brakes just when his tire hit the loose gravel, and this caused him to lose control of the scooter. Before he knew what was happening, Bruce found himself and the bike on the shoulder of the road. Bruce hit the ground hard and slid across the gravel and a portion of the asphalt.

He landed on his left side; he lost most of the tissue on his right leg and left arm. The impact also caused serious abrasions on his cheek and chin. The big toe on his right foot was broken. The metal sunglasses worn to shield his eyes became an instrument of destruction when the metal frames twisted and gouged holes in the side of his head.

Bruce was dazed and barely able to stand as he tried unsuccessfully to set the scooter upright. He was disoriented and was not aware of the extent of his injuries. Bruce looked up and saw a man jogging toward him. The man asked him if he was all right then said to Bruce, "You don't look so good; you really need to go to the hospital!"

Bruce asked the man if he knew of a place where he could clean up from the accident. The man said yes. He then set the scooter upright and instructed Bruce to climb on the back and to hold on around his waist.

The next thing Bruce knew, he was on the ground again! As he regained consciousness, he realized he was not alone! The stranger was standing over him, lightly tapping his face in an effort to bring him around. Bruce passed out when his body went into shock! He was extremely thankful when he discovered the kind stranger had already stopped a passing pickup truck and loaded the scooter into the back of the truck. The man instructed the driver in Spanish to take Bruce to the hospital as he loaded his patient into the cab of the truck. Bruce understood none of the language they spoke except for the word "hospital."

The pain and the blood loss soon alerted Bruce to the fact that he had substantial injuries! He understood the man had probably saved his life when he did not allow him to drive himself on the scooter. He surely would have wrecked when he passed out! Bruce might have died if he had gone off the road into the rugged terrain.

Gratitude flooded Bruce's mind, and he was strongly inclined to thank the man for his kindness and compassion. Bruce did not know his name or how to find the words to thank him. Bruce opened his mouth to say thank you then noticed he was alone except for the truck driver. Bruce looked for the stranger in every direction, but he was nowhere to be found. There was no time for him to run away. He simply vanished! Bruce was amazed when he realized God must have sent an angel to care for him. There was no other explanation because people do not just vanish.

When Bruce arrived back home in Louisiana, he shared the details of the accident and the angel with his wife, Christine. When Christine learned the time of the accident, she recalled her whereabouts at that precise time. The realization was astounding!

Christine previously made a commitment to go to her church to pray with two other women and the pastor. The day of the accident, Christine was at the church praying when the Holy Spirit prompted her to pray for Bruce and for his safety. It was the same time as the accident in Cozumel! She remembered only a soft, still voice urging her to pray for her husband. Obediently, she did pray!

Christine had no way of knowing that God would answer that prayer by sending an angel to care for the man she loved in his hour of need. Bruce and Christine are convinced that divine intervention is real and they know angels appear when we need them. What a comfort it is to know God always watches over His children!

> *O Lord of hosts, how blessed is the man who trusts in You!*
> (Psalm 84:12)

# Chapter 46

# Peaceful Valley

Bill Sims* was a strong and rugged man, inside and out. Through most of his difficult life, he recognized no need for God or His Church. Though his wife was a godly woman with a strong faith, Bill preferred to rely on his own strength. His independent attitude continued unchanged after he suffered a near fatal work-related accident that left him wheelchair-bound for ten years. Now permanently crippled and cane dependent, Bill remained hardened to God's truth even after cancer claimed the life of his son.

Bill was an Ohio native who had moved his family to Florida. Soon after his son's death, Bill decided to return to his hometown for a Christmas visit. Bill's physician advised him to forego the trip. Winters in Ohio are brutally cold and damp, and the doctor was concerned Bill's compromised physical condition would put him at risk for respiratory problems in the harsh, northern climate. True to form, Bill refused to accept his doctor's warning and went on his way to enjoy an Ohio Christmas with his family.

After only a few days in the Ohio winter weather, Bill became extremely ill. He was diagnosed with pneumonia and admitted to the hospital in serious condition. Despite continuous medical attention, Bill's pneumonia worsened. For several days, his physicians fought to save his life. For a brief time, it seemed they would lose the battle—Bill appeared to be more dead than alive.

Bill's physicians were successful in saving his life and Bill recovered from the life-threatening pneumonia. But Bill's life would never be the same. As Bill's doctors fought to save Bill's physical life, Bill had encountered the reality of spiritual existence.

At some point during Bill's battle with pneumonia, Bill visited a different world. He remembers seeing a peaceful valley carpeted with lush, green grass; it was heavenly. There before him was an incredibly beautiful place with towering, elegant trees. As Bill gazed at the idyllic scene, he saw his deceased son walking toward him. A brilliant, white light surrounded him as he approached his dad. Bill's son spoke a simple message in a clear, sure voice, "Go back, Dad. Go back! It's not time for you to come here yet; you have more work to do!"

Bill recovered completely and returned to Florida where he lived for many more years. After his near-death experience, the things of God seemed to have new meaning for him. The experience gave Bill a new perspective on living and dying that led him to find salvation through Jesus Christ. Bill was a changed man with a new and tender heart. He found solace and truth through his son's after-death appearance.

When Bill died many years after his near-death experience, no one doubted he was a saved man who had simply finished his journey on earth and moved on to his heavenly home!

*A fictitious name was used to protect the identity of the deceased.*

Chapter 47

# I'll Fly Away

I met Debbie Matthews, a music executive, one cold, gray November morning. A fine and foggy mist filled the air. My Monday required some rearranging because of an appointment cancellation. I thought of a music business matter I could handle, considering the fact that I suddenly had a free morning. I experienced a holy prompting to go at once! I went online seeking the address for a publishing company then drove toward Nashville with directions on the seat beside me. I headed for 25 Music Square East on Music Row.

Parking places on Music Row are nearly nonexistent, so I decided to find the building then park somewhere in the area and walk back to the business. I located 23 Music Square East but did not see 25 Music Square East. I circled the block a second time; I still did not see the number 25, and no parking space was in sight. I circled the third time and discovered a vacant parking space at the end of a row of parallel-parked cars at 23 Music Square East. I claimed that spot at once and noticed a woman four cars ahead of me, standing outside her car. She appeared to be looking for something.

I approached the woman and made an inquiry about the missing street number, and she smiled and said, "That business has moved. If you will come inside with me, I will help you find the new address." We entered her business called Valhalla Music Group. We exchanged introductions and business cards. She looked at my card and she asked me several questions. When she realized I write about people who have experienced divine intervention in their lives, she said, "I think maybe the Lord sent you to me today!"

Debbie went on to tell me it was her first day back at work after a six-month break. She took the time off to run for a Senate seat. Her run was unsuccessful, and her faith was sorely tested during those months. She was weary from the good, the bad, and the ugly things she encountered in the field of politics. She needed to be reminded that God was real and still in control.

Debbie said, "When I drove into Nashville this morning, I parked outside this building in the very spot where you are now parked. Something told me 'not yet.' I pulled away from the curb and circled the building. When I approached the building the second time, I passed up your parking spot and parked where you found me, then I could not find my keys. I saw the keys as soon as you said, 'Pardon me'."

I laughed and said to Debbie, "God more than likely caused you to do that because He knows I can't parallel park!" I said jokingly, "My insurance company forbids me to do that ever again! God must have hidden your keys until I reached you."

God's timing never ceases to amaze me! God had her park there and save the spot for me then move out of the spot at precisely the right moment so I could park there. God spoke to Debbie and to me that day; we both heard Him and obeyed Him!

We laughed, yet both of us knew our meeting was not by chance! Holy manipulation orchestrated our meeting! I ventured out and asked, "Do you perhaps have a story for my next book?" Debbie smiled and nodded yes. She shared with me the story about her mother's death. Sometimes, the way I get my stories is almost as amazing as the stories!

Debbie's mother, Beverly Jean Chapman, died from Oat Cell Carcinoma of the lungs. She died 15 months after she learned she had cancer.

Beverly's nickname was "Jackie." She was a beautiful person and an elegant woman. Jackie's eyes were green, and her smile was contagious; she never met a stranger. Everyone who knew her loved her. Debbie loved her mom very much.

Early in the morning, on the day of Beverly's death, Debbie left her home in Columbia, Tennessee, to have her hair cut. She left her mom at her home under the care of a hospice nurse. Later that morning Debbie received a call to return home; her mom's death appeared imminent.

Debbie returned home as fast as she could! Many visitors and a minister surrounded her mom, so Debbie asked them to leave the room; she wanted the death experience to be a personal and private matter. Debbie's husband, Jason, and one hospice nurse remained in the room. She asked her singer/songwriter husband to sing, but he couldn't because of the tears. Jason loved his mother-in-law very much; sadness overwhelmed him.

Debbie quickly found a CD and pressed play. The voice of Vern Gosden singing "I'll Fly Away" filled the room with song and praises in a final farewell to Beverly. Everyone joined in and started singing the song! Debbie contemplated the suffering she saw in her mom with lung cancer; then she visualized the heavenly realm she was about to enter. Debbie looked into her mom's beautiful jade green eyes as her mom looked back at her. Her mom communicated without speaking a word. Words poured from Debbie's spirit through her mouth as she affectionately cried out to her mother, "Run, Jackie, run!"

At that moment, Debbie saw with her eyes her mom's spirit actually leaving her body. A white mist, a white sweeping vapor, soared from her body then swirled upward and away from her motionless body. The spirit appeared to be running! Debbie never questioned the experience; she felt great comfort from what she saw. There was no fear! She knew her devout Christian mother was now completely healed and Heaven-bound!

*...He will dwell among them, and they shall be His people, and God Himself will be among them, and He will wipe away every tear from their eyes; and there will no longer be any death; there will no longer be any mourning, or crying, or pain; the first things have passed away* (Revelation 21:3-4).

# Chapter 48

# Miraculous Trilogy

## PART ONE

Although the Vietnam War still raged abroad, Danny Kellum enlisted in the Army immediately after he graduated from college. Soon after completing Officer Candidate School, he was ordered to active duty in Vietnam. Danny was a newlywed and struggled to tell his young wife he would soon be leaving. His wife feared he would die in combat, but Danny was committed and courageous. He came from a long line of patriots; he was ready to serve his country, no matter the cost.

Danny's company was deployed. Danny served as a Forward Observer for the 101st Airborne Division, assigned to Alpha Company, the second of the 502nd Infantry. Their mission was "search and destroy." This meant they were sent into a particular area by helicopter with orders to destroy the enemy before the enemy destroyed them. Fear and anxiety were constant companions for Alpha Company and its Forward Observer.

With incredible clarity, Danny recalls a particular mission. Alpha Company had been in the same location for ten days, a strange departure from protocol, which required relocation every 24 hours. Danny remembers, "We were in the mountainous jungles of South Vietnam securing a location that overlooked the Song Bo River. During that time, we were interdicting enemy concentration in the area. Through intercepted enemy communication, we discovered that our position was going to be overrun by the enemy that night." Alpha Company would have to move out.

Believing there were enemy soldiers just outside the area, Danny's platoon waited for darkness to begin the search for a safe place to spend the night. No flashlights aided their search; they navigated through the black night with only the guide of a compass. Unable to locate an elevated place where gravity would make defense easier (it is a much simpler task to throw hand grenades downhill), they took refuge in a low-lying area.

Later that evening, an artillery barrage was mounted against the recently vacated location, now overrun by the enemy. The night was pitch black, making accurate targeting of the area nearly impossible. In an effort to direct the artillery, a smoke round from World War II was fired into the air above the vicinity of the enemy's location. Both rounds failed to explode and crashed to the earth. Although Danny could not see the smoke, he heard the round's impact. Using the sound as his guide, Danny fired two rounds of high explosives toward the target. One round went off unexpectedly close. The explosion was only a few feet away from where Danny and his troops were located; however, Danny and his troops were totally unscathed.

Danny says, "I still don't know what happened that night, but that round almost killed us." As Danny relates the circumstances of his brush with death, it is obvious he is convinced that divine intervention saved his life.

## PART TWO

Two days later, Danny's platoon had made its way to a clearing atop a hill, a makeshift landing zone for helicopters. From that position, Danny began to shoot artillery toward the enemy's location.

"As I stood there, I heard a piece of shrapnel coming at us," said Danny. "A bullet makes a whistling sound; shrapnel makes a chirping sound. You can't see shrapnel coming any more than you can see a bullet coming at you; they move at the same speed. It was singing through the air. I decided to stand very still and let it miss me. It did not miss me. It hit me in the heart area of my chest! I was knocked on the ground. It cut and bruised me, but it didn't kill me."

Later Danny held the piece of shrapnel up against his chest and had his radiotelephone operator take a picture. The shrapnel was almost five inches long and nearly two inches wide, a jagged hunk of metal that looked like it was ripped from a solid sheet of steel. Mistakenly, the roll of film containing the photo was sent to his wife. She wrote Danny asking what that was in his hand against his chest. He neglected to answer her question in his next letter. Only when he was safely home did he tell her the real story about how God saved him from certain death!

Danny now recalls, "If that piece of shrapnel had been turned another fraction of an inch, or had I moved another fraction of an inch, if I had tried to dodge a fraction of an inch, it would have gone through me and taken out my heart and lungs instantly!

"I reached down and picked it up, then got down on my knees and thanked God for sparing my life. As a believer, I knew that I was alive because God Himself had protected me; He had positioned me perfectly still. Then He positioned that piece of shrapnel in such a way that it broadsided me instead of slicing through me." Danny has never doubted that, once again, divine intervention protected him from death.

## Part Three

It has been about 40 years since Danny Kellum began his tour of duty in the Army. Second Lieutenant Danny Kellum is now Dr. Kellum.

He served as the Headmaster of Donelson Christian Academy, a private Christian school in Nashville, Tennessee, for many years.

His present lifestyle is much different from the life-threatening conditions of an Artillery Forward Observer. God's protective love is still active in Dr. Kellum's life; divine intervention is still a fact in this grateful man's experience.

A few years ago, Dr. Kellum was assisting in the disassembly of a large scaffold that had been used during graduation to hold a huge drapery. One piece of scaffolding had been disengaged and lowered to the ground. Dr. Kellum worked to loosen the next section. Suddenly, he lost his footing and fell 24 feet to the gymnasium floor! His body struck the scaffolding many times before he landed heavily, his back and head crashing with great force into the solid, wooden surface.

Dr. Kellum remained conscious after the fall. He even remembers hearing a student call 911 for assistance. He was taken by ambulance to the emergency room of Vanderbilt Medical Center. Dr. Kellum was thoroughly examined due to the distance and impact of his fall. A number of scrapes and bruises were found, but Dr. Kellum had miraculously escaped any serious injury. He walked out of the emergency room that same day!

"It was a miraculous event from God," said Dr. Kellum. His life had been spared once again.

## Epilogue

Dr. Kellum is able to look back over many, many years with genuine gratitude toward God, still giving Him all the glory for each time his life has been spared.

Dr. Kellum has a daughter, Deeannah, and two sons, Dan and Rob. Both of his sons have served in the U.S. Military. The advice Dr. Kellum offered his sons before they deployed was this: "Be faithful and true to God. Make sure you share your faith with others. There will always be people who are looking and searching for answers to life and life's questions; Jesus is the answer. Others need to hear your testimony to be able to fully understand your relationship to God. Do not think people will observe your lives and see Jesus. You must share the Gospel."

Chapter 49

# The Hazy Lady

Marilyn Halpin was only 12 years old when she moved with her parents and little brother from Washington State to Goose Bay, Labrador. Labrador is a province of Canada on the country's Atlantic coast in northeastern North America. This easternmost Canadian Province comprises two main parts: the island of Newfoundland off the country's east coast, and Labrador on the mainland to the northwest of the island. Newfoundland and Labrador's motto is *Quaerite primum regnum Dei*. In English, this means: *Seek ye first the kingdom of God* (Matt. 6:33 KJV).

The nearest town was Labrador City, and it was 300 miles away! Marilyn's father, commanding officer Major John Halpin, was a helicopter pilot in the USAF when he and his family moved to Goose Bay. They lived in an apartment building with a basement and two upper stories. The snow got above the first story of the dwelling! Twelve feet of snow was average there, and darkness prevailed 3 months out of 12.

When Major Halpin was initially stationed to the Canadian Outpost, housing was not available for his family. That was a common dilemma. At the last minute, housing suddenly became available, and he was able to move his family with him. Marilyn did not learn the reason for this until years later!

In 1959, 12-year-old Marilyn experienced an extraordinary visit from a woman who was not of this world. Marilyn's dad was away so her mom came into her bedroom to sleep next to her that night. Marilyn's mom, Inez, was sound asleep, but Marilyn could not sleep. She lay awake, thinking about northern lights, icebergs, and 12 feet of snow outside! A small night light illumined the darkness. The vast amount of snow outside created a silence and stillness unlike anything Marilyn had ever known.

Suddenly, Marilyn saw something move and looked up to see a woman standing near the bed looking at her! The woman was translucent; Marilyn could see her clearly. The woman did not walk; she floated as a foggy haze but appeared clearly visible as a woman. Marilyn noticed details. The hazy lady wore a long dress, and Marilyn could see the folds of the fabric of her clothing move as the woman moved. She had long flowing hair.

The woman smiled and gazed intently at Marilyn; Marilyn experienced no fear, and she was not apprehensive.

"She took my breath away! I was not afraid even as she leaned over and motioned with her hand for me to come with her. I just stared at her; I could not take my eyes off her! Finally, I buried my face in my mother's back for several minutes before I opened my eyes to see if she was still there. She was still there, looking at me. I was frozen! The woman appeared saddened when I did not go with her as she beckoned to me," exclaimed Marilyn. "She moved from her original position and repositioned herself at the window where she stood looking out for a very long time."

The woman looked over her shoulder at Marilyn with a sad expression on her face. It sent chills over Marilyn! She buried her face in her mother's back once again. About 20 minutes passed from start to finish. Marilyn looked one last time, and the woman looked at Marilyn one last time before she began floating toward the door. She left the room, never to be seen again.

Marilyn was a young Catholic girl who was enamored with nuns. She wanted to be a nun when she grew up. She earnestly thought about the woman and wondered if she was the Virgin Mary. This strange woman did not cause fear; quite the contrary, Marilyn felt a holy sense of awe while in her presence.

The second year Marilyn lived in that home, she had a very serious accident. She was playing while wearing her mother's high heels one day. She accidentally fell down the steep, carpeted stairs that led from the second floor bedroom to the carpeted living room floor. Marilyn injured her neck and back. To this day, she suffers from neck and back pain from that nearly fatal fall.

Marilyn learned much later that the sudden availability of housing came because of the death of the previous occupant. The occupant was a young woman who died when she fell down the steep wood stairs from the kitchen to the basement concrete floor. She was hosting a party that fateful night.

Marilyn will never know for sure if her unearthly visitor was an angel from Heaven or the spirit of the woman who fell to her death before they moved into the Goose Bay home. Looking back, Marilyn believes the holy being came to warn her so she would use caution when near the stairs that proved to be a death trap.

When Marilyn shared her story with me, tears flowed freely down her face as we talked. I was amazed to hear her describe the appearance because I witnessed Marilyn laughing with an inexpressible joy when she recalled the holy appearance while tears filled her eyes and drenched her face. She laughed and cried simultaneously during her remembrance. I told her I had never heard such sweet and joyful laughter.

I can only believe the holy being was an angel who came to warn Marilyn about the dangerous place where a child might be inclined to play in high heels. I believe God sent the angel to protect from harm an innocent child who focused her thoughts on the Virgin Mary and serving as a nun for His Kingdom.

> *Do not neglect to show hospitality to strangers, for by this some have entertained angels without knowing it* (Hebrews 13:2).

# Chapter 50

# What Do You Believe?

Pastor Alton Parker* was a Missionary Baptist minister from a small rural town near Nashville, Tennessee. He was a godly man, sincerely devoted to serving the Lord. He was highly regarded and respected by his parishioners.

Without warning, Pastor Parker suffered a stroke that left him severely impaired. Following extensive tests, it was discovered Pastor Parker had a significant blockage of the right carotid artery, the main blood vessel leading to the right side of the brain. Since the right side of the brain controls the left side of the body, the stroke had left Pastor Parker with his left side paralyzed, hopefully a temporary condition.

Dr. Arthur Cushman, a neurosurgeon in Nashville, recommended Pastor Parker undergo a carotid endarterectomy, a procedure to remove the fatty buildup of plaque from his carotid artery. Pastor Parker agreed, and he entered the hospital for the procedure.

The surgery was uneventful and the surgery team prepared to take Pastor Parker to post-operative care. They had just disconnected the anesthetic when Pastor Parker's blood pressure began to climb to a potentially lethal level. Fearing a brain hemorrhage would result, the anesthetist quickly administered intravenous medication to lower Pastor Parker's dangerous blood pressure. The medication worked too well. His pressure dropped to zero and his heart nearly stopped. The operating team worked frantically, giving him CPR and successfully resuscitated him. Pastor Parker survived and suffered no ill effects from the surgery.

The next day in the Intensive Care Unit, Pastor Parker requested a private conversation with Dr. Cushman. The nurse left the room and he asked, "I died at the end of the surgery, didn't I?" He continued, "My soul floated out of my body, and I watched as the resuscitation was going on." Reverend Parker was able to accurately and precisely describe the series of events that had taken place. He told Dr. Cushman exactly where he and each member of the operating team was standing and what they said during those critical moments. The accuracy of his account stunned and amazed Dr. Cushman.

"I traveled through a long, dark tunnel where I had a review of my entire life!" said Pastor Parker. "When I reached the end of the tunnel, I approached a beautiful bright light and a beautiful land! I saw Jesus and the angels. I saw many of my family members who died years ago. All of my loved ones looked very young and vigorous. Brilliant white light surrounded each individual. My deceased loved ones came to greet me, and it was like a family reunion! It was all so wonderful; I just wanted to stay there. I came back only because Jesus told me I had to. He said it was not time for me to die."

Accompanied by angels, the pastor returned to his body and woke up in the recovery room. When he awoke, he felt wonderful and filled with extreme peace. He was no longer afraid of dying.

Pastor Parker told Dr. Cushman, "My church does not believe this can happen. They believe there is no separation of body, soul, and spirit. They believe all die together and await the resurrection when Jesus comes back." Pastor Parker had no idea how he would tell his church about his near-death experience.

Dr. Cushman then took his hand and said, "Thank you, Brother Parker. What do you believe?" In answer, Pastor Parker just smiled a knowing smile, quite confident about what had happened to him and where he had been!

*A fictitious name was used to protect the identity of the patient.*

# Chapter 51

# Angels Do Sing in Heaven

The last day of January was cold and snowy in Mexico, Missouri, but the winter weather did not deter Tina Groves. She home-schooled her two children, so the kids looked forward to seeing their friends on frequent outings. That day they planned to go to their church home school group for gym and art classes at 1:30 in the afternoon. They journeyed safely through the snow to the church and back home at 5:30. A nagging feeling in the back of Tina's mind persisted. For some reason, the day seemed strange. Tina could not identify her feelings; she only knew something felt different in her spirit.

Tina's mom called shortly after she got home and expressed concern because she could not reach Tina's dad by phone. The two were divorced when Tina was only 14 years old; however, they remained friends and talked to each other every day. Tina suddenly identified her heightened spiritual awareness. She was experiencing a sense of unidentifiable loss! In her heart, Tina somehow knew her dad was dead. I believe the Holy Spirit prepares God's children when there is a need.

The police department in Auxrasse, Missouri, sent a policeman to the home of Charles Stone, and the officer confirmed Tina's suspicions. Her dad apparently died suddenly from a heart attack early that morning during his devotion time. Each morning Mr. Stone got up and fixed a pot of coffee, smoked his pipe, and read his Bible. After that, he routinely fed his birds, fish, and rabbits. He didn't get to finish his coffee that January day.

Years of stored-up memories and emotions flooded Tina's mind. She thought about who her dad was as a person. First and foremost, he was a Christian! He lived 74 years as a very private man of few words. He loved God, people, and animals. Mr. Stone worshiped in God's house and taught his family to do likewise. He sought the Lord in prayer and read his Bible daily. Charles Stone was a singer of songs, and he often hummed or whistled the tunes to favorite hymns such as "Amazing Grace," "May the Circle be Unbroken," and "The Old Rugged Cross." Music was an important part of his life.

Later in the evening, Tina walked into her little girl's room to turn the bedcovers down. She was all alone when she gave in to her sorrow and allowed the tears to flow; she wept in silence. Tina was not prepared to let go of her dad. She missed him, and her heart was filled with regret because they did not have the opportunity to say good-bye.

A voice suddenly interrupted Tina's solitude. Tina's deceased father actually spoke to her with his strong voice. She did not see her dad, but his voice was undeniable and unmistakable! He called her by her nickname. He clearly said to her, "Tina-o-girl, the angels really do sing in Heaven!" Tina stood speechless and amazed that God allowed her dad to communicate with her from Heaven. The heaviness in her heart dissipated at once!

Tina reflects on that after-death experience by saying, "At that moment I knew my father was fine, and he was with our heavenly Father! Praise God for the day I will see him again! Until that time, I know he will be singing with the angels!"

> *As for the days of our life, they contain seventy years, or if due to strength, eighty years...* (Psalm 90:10).

# Chapter 52

# Changed

At the age of 76, Kelly Turner received a startling diagnosis: He was in the final stage of lung cancer. A kind and simple man who had grown up in the country, Mr. Turner was seriously ill-at-ease in city settings and detested hospitals. However, he wisely decided to overcome his hesitancy; he was admitted to the hospital in Oak Ridge, Tennessee, for chemotherapy.

Understandably, Mr. Turner struggled with the knowledge of his impending death. He had many visitors and enjoyed their company, but the dire prognosis caused a pall to overshadow every visit.

Before Mr. Turner's chemotherapy could begin, it was necessary for minor surgery to be performed to insert an access port into an artery. Mr. Turner was lightly sedated during the procedure; he tolerated it well, and there were no complications. After the completion of the procedure, Mr. Turner was brought back to his room. It was obvious that something about him had changed.

After the procedure, Mr. Turner's sad, somber countenance was replaced by a joyous attitude! Mr. Turner smiled a radiant smile; he seemed overjoyed and elated. When his family questioned him about the change that had come over him, Mr. Turner explained, "I have been with Jesus! He told me I am going to be all right and everything is going to be OK!"

Mr. Turner told his family he had visited Heaven during the surgical procedure; he had seen Jesus! He reported having seen many deceased loved ones during his time with the Lord; strangely, he had also seen his daughter, Virginia.

Virginia was quite obviously alive and well, and found her father's report quite perplexing. Though her dad was certain of the reality of his near-death encounter, Virginia struggled to understand her own presence in the vision. Being prone to worry and anxiety, Virginia found herself a bit uneasy. Finally, she came to realize her dad had actually seen into the future—to a time when they would, indeed, be together in the Kingdom of God.

Mr. Turner's near-death encounter left him with a lasting euphoria. He maintained his good spirits throughout his remaining days. Mr. Turner died one month after his heavenly vision.

Virginia had been especially close to her dad and found it extremely hard to deal with his death. She spent many sleepless nights struggling to find peace and acceptance.

One night, about a week after her father's death, Virginia failed to find much-needed sleep. As she lay in bed, wide-awake, her father appeared in her bedroom. He was only a couple of feet away, leaning against the dresser close to the foot of her bed. He was wearing jeans and a golden-tan, striped shirt. He looked vibrant and healthy!

Mr. Turner spoke to his daughter, "Gin, you need to stop worrying and don't be afraid. It is all right to acknowledge the things that bother you; however, you must learn to let those things go." As suddenly as he appeared, he vanished.

Virginia turned on the light and got out of the bed, reasoning with herself about what she had just experienced. She was not dreaming; she was wide-awake. Though she could not explain the strange occurrence, she was not upset or frightened. Her worry and anxiety seemed to have evaporated; she was no longer concerned about her dad!

After her father's visit, Virginia began to experience a newfound peace; not only was her concern about her father gone, she discovered her predisposition to worry and fret had quieted and her fearful heart had stilled. It seemed quite clear to Virginia that her dad's after-death appearance was an attempt to impart a message to her. Was he trying to say, "Hold onto faith, let go of fear"?

In the time that has passed since her dad's visit, Virginia has learned to release fear and worry, maintaining a calm, trusting, inner confidence. She came away from the experience with the certain knowledge of God's love and presence and an enduring sense of peace.

# Chapter 53

# No Earthly Way

Glen Hanks is a gifted computer specialist. He graciously agreed to work on my laptop one Saturday morning after a virus erased all of my computer data. We sat in his home office and talked as he worked. We discussed current events, Christmas, and childhood stories. Glen's story about his childhood touched my heart!

"Imagine being a seven-year-old second grader," Glen suggested to me. "A car filled with total strangers drives up to your door and one of the strangers says, 'Get your things together, you're going with me.' I put everything I owned in two brown paper sacks. We drove away that day, and I left my whole world behind!"

Until that day, Glen spent most of his young life in the home of his beloved grandmother, Trannie Key. She was half Cherokee; she was a devout Christian who did her best to care for her three young grandsons in the absence of responsible parents. She raised the boys for as long as she could. Trannie taught Glen and his two brothers many things. She taught them about God. Glen possessed a vast knowledge about geography and history by the age of 5. His grandmother was a natural-born teacher. She instilled in him the desire to learn. Glen and Trannie shared an unusual spiritual connection.

Glen's journey through life was not easy. He was adopted twice and lived in more than a dozen foster homes until he was old enough to join the United States Navy.

At the age of 19, Glen traveled back home to Monterey, Tennessee, and he located Trannie in a nursing home. A nurse escorted him to Trannie's room, and they stood at the door a moment and observed her sitting at her writing desk. The nurse said, "Mrs. Key, you have a guest!"

Trannie stopped writing and slowly placed her pen down; she spoke before she ever turned her head. She exclaimed, "Glen, I always knew you would come back to see me!"

Glen exclaimed, "Grandma, how did you know I was here?"

She replied, "I just know!"

The two hugged each other and their spirits connected once again. Glen felt that same sweet and unconditional love he once experienced as a small child. The visit was incredible!

In the years to come, Glen's naval career carried him to more than 40 countries. His IQ of 197 enabled him to accomplish more than he ever dreamed he possibly could! In 1987, Glen was onboard a ship in the Indian Ocean when he was filled with an uncanny knowing. He stopped in his tracks; he stood perfectly still as the Holy Spirit of God somehow connected his soul with the soul of his beloved grandmother thousands of miles away. Glen just knew!

Glen's buddy asked him what was going on. Glen couldn't explain, but he was keenly aware that part of him was gone. He experienced an overwhelming sense of loss. Glen replied, "My grandmother just died!" There was no earthly way he could have known.

Glen received confirmation later that day by way of Red Cross that Trannie was dead; she had indeed crossed over from this world into her heavenly home.

*I will meditate on all Your work and muse on Your deeds.*
*Your way, O God, is holy; what god is great like our God?*
(Psalm 77:12-13)

# Chapter 54

# Gracie's Journey

Gracie followed her brother Gage into this world as the second child of loving parents, Tina and Bruce Bentley. She was born with soft, platinum-blonde hair and lovely blue eyes. Tina was an affectionate and attentive mother. She expressed concern to Gracie's doctor when Gracie developed gastrointestinal problems. The symptoms were not easily treatable. Before Christmastime, the illness progressed alarmingly and three-month-old Gracie ended up in Vanderbilt Medical Center in Nashville.

The doctors discovered Gracie suffered from a rare disorder known as Hirschsprung's disease and a severe intestinal infection. Hirschsprung's disease is a result of a birth defect that affects sections of the large intestine by the absence of normal nerve cells. The intestine cannot function without the nerve cells.

Nine-pound Gracie endured a risky surgery to remove a section of her infected colon. The tiny baby recovered and her parents carried her home from the hospital wearing a colostomy bag strapped to her side.

The doctor scheduled reconstructive surgery for six months later. Tina grew extremely anxious about the approaching surgical procedure. Somehow, in her spirit, Tina sensed something terribly wrong was ahead of them!

Gracie survived the second surgery needed to reconstruct her colon and reverse the colostomy. Several hours after the procedure, Gracie's body began convulsing; she did not respond to the drugs she received for pain. A doctor performed an epidural, a delicate procedure involving an injection into the epidural space of the spine, intended to block pain sensations. The procedure failed. Nurses administered morphine, a strong painkiller, and Valium, a potent drug used for anxiety and uncontrollable muscle movements; however, there was no relief for the traumatized infant.

The night progressed and Gracie's frail body finally relaxed. Close to three o'clock in the morning, a nurse entered the room and injected Valium into Gracie's IV port. Mother's intuition compelled Tina to question the nurse and oppose the injection; however, the nurse dispensed the drug in accordance to orders on the patient's chart. Suddenly, Gracie's breathing changed. Her respiration decreased, her lips swelled and turned blue, and then she stopped breathing. The infant's weakened body could not tolerate any more of the drug, and her system responded by simply shutting down.

The concerned nurse called a code and nurses scrambled into the room; Gracie's death was imminent! Tina was in the bed with Gracie on her hands and knees. She lifted Gracie's lifeless body, holding her lengthwise in front of her own body while nurses worked frantically to reconnect the disconnected IV line. Counteractive measures were impossible until the IV was in place again. Tina looked into the face of a male nurse and desperately questioned, "What do I do?" He replied, "You holding her is doing more than anything we can do for her now." Tina understood that Gracie was dying.

Tina recalled her own experience like this. "I was no longer in that room; in my spirit, I went somewhere else. All the voices in the room grew silent. I was not aware of others around me, only a peaceful feeling transporting me to the blessed solitude of oneness with God. I felt like I went straight to the feet of Jesus. I prayed so hard! I have never prayed that way before or since! My plea came from the depths of my soul! I was with God and He was with me. I was begging Him to spare my baby's life, to let us please keep her! I knew I had God and nothing else was going to help. *Nothing else could help!*"

The medical team worked diligently to resuscitate Gracie. Tina said, "I remember when I first became vaguely aware of my surroundings again. A nurse was staring into my face, asking if I was all right. I regained my sight and I could read her lips but I could not hear her voice. Slowly, I regained my senses." Tina fought a life-or-death battle for Gracie's life that night! Tina's weapon was prayer! God's love and power produced a mighty miracle and restored Gracie's life. Gracie, Tina, and Bruce survived that grueling night. The doctors sent Gracie home to recuperate after seven days.

More than two years passed; Gracie miraculously recovered and grew into a healthy child with an exceptionally sweet spirit! One day Tina sat reading a book to Gracie. The book title was *My Little Book About God.* Gracie began asking questions about the scar on her tummy and Tina told her the scar was a reminder of what God did for her when she was a baby.

Little Gracie replied to her mom, "I know...I saw God when I was a baby!" Tina was taken aback and she told Gracie she wanted to hear more, being careful not to say anything to influence her. Gracie continued, "You and Daddy were there, Mommy, and you were holding me in a bed...like this." Gracie extended her arms in front of her, exactly the same way Tina held Gracie that night as her life faded away.

"I looked down and I saw you. Daddy was over there beside the bed." Gracie pointed her finger and beamed as she spoke, saying, "God was sitting in a great big chair and He was holding me and hugging me and loving me! I want to go back to see God, and I want you and Daddy to go too!"

Tina never told three-year-old Gracie the details of that terrible night. In fact, she shielded her from the suffering she endured. How could Gracie possibly know the details of that night? Tina trembled as Gracie innocently shared details of her journey. Tears of sincere, heartfelt gratitude filled Tina's eyes. Chills ran through her body as she acknowledged the miracles that occurred on that memorable night. Tina's grief turned to pure joy!

Presently, when 11-year-old Gracie smiles, a light radiates from within! Her gentle disposition is obvious and her characteristics resemble those of an angel! I shared an afternoon with Gracie and her adorable little sister, Lainey, getting to know them. Gracie exudes the fruit of the spirit: *love, joy, peace, patience, kindness, goodness, faithfulness, gentleness, and self-control* as described in the Book of Galatians 5:22 and 23.

Tina and Bruce claim they are not the same people as before; their lives changed forever. They are closer to God and their faith is much stronger since Gracie's near-death experience. Tina explained, "For those who have babies in Heaven, I only hope they can be comforted and encouraged by Gracie's experience. If God held Gracie in that big chair, if He hugged her and loved her, surely He has held their babies in that same big chair, in His loving arms, as He welcomed them home."

# Chapter 55

# Holy Water

Michael Griffin, a close family friend and neighbor, often helped me at our farm after my husband, Burke, passed away. In early spring, my large mower needed service. Michael and I talked as he prepared to load the mower onto his trailer. Michael was very fond of Burke and we reminisced about some of the happy times they experienced.

As Michael prepared to leave, he flashed a big grin before he proudly told me the news! He and his wife, Alison, were expecting their first child!

That exciting news reminded me of the dream I had the night before, and I said to Michael, "I dreamed of Burke last night and in the dream, he mentioned your baby!" I asked Burke, "What are you doing here?" He replied, "I've come to bring holy water for Michael's baby."

My deceased husband spoke those words as we stood in a vast dining room filled with men and women who appeared to be between the ages of 30 and 40 years old. They were all smiling and appeared to be genuinely happy as they engaged in lively conversations.

I finished speaking and I looked at Michael. He stood very still, with a strange look on his face. After a long pause, Michael spoke, saying, "We received a bottle of holy water for the baby from a family friend three days ago! It came in the mail."

I felt a tingling sensation flow up and down my arms, as if the hairs were standing on end! I realized something out of the ordinary was happening and something supernatural had happened to get the holy water from Lourdes, France' to a small town in Tennessee! Burke's after-death appearance in the dream could only mean the holy water was heaven-sent for a specific reason.

Almost three years passed before Michael and I conversed about the holy water incident again. Michael and Alison's healthy baby had grown into a healthy toddler. The child appeared to possess intelligence and perception well beyond his years. Rosy cheeks, soft red curls rimming his tiny face, and an angelic smile melted my heart when I first saw him. I wondered what special purpose God had in store for this extraordinary little boy!

One day, I decided to discuss the holy water dream with Alison and she told me an interesting story about her pregnancy. Alison suggested that I talk to her friend, Maggie Dyer of Gilbertsville, Pennsylvania. Maggie was the woman who sent the holy water. I asked Maggie what prompted her to mail the holy water from Lourdes for the baby. Maggie sent the holy water after a conversation with Alison's mom, Diane, who expressed concern for the unborn baby. An ultrasound report indicated the possibility of an abnormality with one kidney and the heart. Michael had not mentioned the abnormalities at the time of our conversation.

Alison, Diane' and Maggie prayed that God would heal the baby and Alison decided to accept the baby as God gave him; he would be perfect in her eyes, no matter what. Alison rubbed the water on her stomach as Maggie suggested and she believed her baby was healed!

The baby was born in July and he arrived in good health, normal and perfect in every way!

God is not far from us. He hears every whispered prayer and He went to great lengths to send holy drops of water from France to Pennsylvania to Tennessee for a precious baby the doctors referred to as "a fetus."

[God said,] *Before I formed you in the womb I knew you...* (Jeremiah 1:5).

*Note: Sick people have traveled to Lourdes, France, since 1858, when a young French girl, acting in obedience to visions she had of the Virgin Mary, dug a hole in the earth, releasing a miraculous spring that produced healing water. The initial few drops of water multiplied until a spring emerged! When the nuns at Lourdes bathed the sick and dying in the water, they got well! Millions of visitors go to Lourdes each year in search of the holy water, associated with thousands of supernatural cures over the years.*

# Prayer of Salvation

*If you confess with your mouth, "Jesus is Lord," and believe in your heart that God raised Him from the dead, you will be saved* (Romans 10:9 NIV).

Here is an idea of what you might want to pray to God. It is a personal petition from you to God.

*Dear God,*

*I know I have broken Your laws and my sins have separated me from You. I am truly sorry, and now I turn away from my past sinful life toward You. Please forgive me, and help me avoid sinning again. I believe Your Son, Jesus Christ, died for my sins, was resurrected from the dead, and He is alive today. I invite Jesus to become the Lord of my life from this day forward. Please help me live a meaningful and purposeful life until You call me home to be with You in Heaven someday. Thank You, Lord.*

*In Jesus' name I pray, amen.*

# Afterword

I am very interested in hearing from readers who would care to share their near-death experiences, after-death appearances, heavenly messages, angelic encounters, miraculous answers to prayer, and stories about divine intervention.

You may contact me at Stories@DavisJacksonPublishers.com. Tell me about your experience, in your own words and simply stated, to give me an idea of what happened. If I am interested in your experience, I will contact you for an interview. I will write your story in my own words, based on what you tell me. I do not include any stories written by others in my books. Thank you!

# In the right hands, This Book will Change Lives!

Most of the people who need this message will not be looking for this book. To change their lives, you need to put a copy of this book in their hands.

> *But others (seeds) fell into good ground, and brought forth fruit, some a hundred-fold, some sixty-fold, some thirty-fold* (Matthew 13:8).

Our ministry is constantly seeking methods to find the good ground, the people who need this anointed message to change their lives. Will you help us reach these people?

> *Remember this—a farmer who plants only a few seeds will get a small crop. But the one who plants generously will get a generous crop* (2 Corinthians 9:6).

## EXTEND THIS MINISTRY BY SOWING
3 BOOKS, 5 BOOKS, 10 BOOKS, **OR MORE TODAY**,
AND BECOME A LIFE CHANGER!

Thank you,

Don Nori Sr., Founder
Destiny Image
Since 1982

# DESTINY IMAGE PUBLISHERS, INC.

*"Promoting Inspired Lives."*

## VISIT OUR NEW SITE HOME AT
## WWW.DESTINYIMAGE.COM

## FREE SUBSCRIPTION TO DI NEWSLETTER

Receive free unpublished articles by top DI authors, exclusive
discounts, and free downloads from our best and newest books.
**Visit www.destinyimage.com to subscribe.**

Write to:       Destiny Image
                P.O. Box 310
                Shippensburg, PA 17257-0310

Call:       1-800-722-6774

Email:       orders@destinyimage.com

For a complete list of our titles or to place an order
online, visit www.destinyimage.com.

FIND US ON FACEBOOK OR FOLLOW US ON TWITTER.

www.facebook.com/destinyimage       facebook
www.twitter.com/destinyimage       twitter